The Sublime Pleasures of Tragedy

The Sublime Pleasures of Tragedy

A Study of Critical Theory
from Dennis to Keats

W. P. ALBRECHT

THE UNIVERSITY PRESS OF KANSAS
Lawrence / Manhattan / Wichita

© Copyright 1975 by the University Press of Kansas
Printed in the United States of America
Designed by Yvonne Willingham

Library of Congress Cataloging in Publication Data
Albrecht, William Price, 1907-
    The sublime pleasures of tragedy.

    Bibliography: p.
    1. Sublime, The. 2. Tragedy—History and
    criticism. 3. Pleasure. 4. Tragic, The.
I. Title.
BH301.S8A4   820'.9'16   75-11896
ISBN 0-7006-0135-X

To

My Wife

PREFACE

The history of the sublime in English literature has been treated comprehensively and in detail, while the pleasures of tragedy as disclosed by English criticism have received equally admirable attention. However, as far as I know, the use of the sublime to explain why tragic materials give pleasure has not been examined in any systematic way. The merger of the sublime and the tragic took place during the eighteenth and early nineteenth centuries, completing itself in the definitions of sublimity and tragedy offered by Hazlitt and Keats. In the meantime, criticism was entrusting new powers to the imagination, and it is in light of these powers that this study attempts to explain the union of tragedy and sublimity.

One cannot write on the sublime without gratefully acknowledging the studies by Professors Samuel H. Monk, David B. Morris, Marjorie Nicolson, and Walter J. Hipple, Jr., or on the pleasures of tragedy as seen in the seventeenth and eighteenth centuries without a similar acknowledgment to Professors Earl R. Wasserman and Eric Rothstein. In addition, of course, I am indebted to many other scholars who have written on English literary history and criticism. My notes can only partially recognize this debt.

Earlier versions of chapters 1, 5, and 8 appeared, respectively, in *Studies on Voltaire and the Eighteenth Century* 82 (1972):65–85; *Romantic and Victorian: Studies in Memory of William H. Marshall,* ed. W. Paul Elledge and Richard L. Hoffman (Rutherford, N.J.: Fairleigh Dickinson University Press, 1971); and *The Nineteenth Century Writer and His Audience,* ed. Harold Orel and George J. Worth (Lawrence, Kans., 1969). For permission to reprint these chapters I am grateful to Professor Theodore Besterman of the Voltaire Foundation, to the Associated University Presses, and to the University of Kansas Humanities Studies.

I am also grateful to the University of Kansas for a sabbatical leave and for some research grants that enabled me to work on this project; to Professors W. D. Paden and Richard L. Eversole, who read portions of the manuscript; to other colleagues and students at the University of Kansas with whom I discussed parts of the book; to my research assistant, William Hatcher; and to the staffs of the Cambridge University Library, the British Museum, and the University of Kansas Libraries.

W. P. ALBRECHT

Lawrence
25 January 1975

CONTENTS

Contents

INTRODUCTION

THE SUBLIME
AND THE TRAGIC

Painful materials become pleasing in a work of art, but
why they do has been a problem of long standing. Writers on
tragedy continue to give frequent and varied answers. Confronting the question in 1817, Keats wrote that "all disagreeables evaporate from their being in close relationship with
Beauty & Truth." By the time Keats made this remark about
King Lear, the imagination had been endowed with considerable power. It could bring all the resources of the mind into
the creative act and fuse sensation, emotion, and thought in
the immediate impact of a work of art. Early in the eighteenth century, however, the imagination was regarded as a
mere picture-making faculty, with little to offer in the way of
serious knowledge. In extending its pleasures to account for
those materials that, outside a work of art, would be disagreeable, English criticism proceeded but slowly toward the answer we find in Keats and, before him, in Hazlitt.

There were available, of course, a number of answers
inherited from the seventeenth century. Why tragedy pleases
has always been a perplexing question because tragedy deals
with evil and terror, subjects not generally considered pleas-

1

ant. The seventeenth century found its most emphatic answer in tragedy's corroboration of an ethical system: tragedy depicts characters admirable in resisting evil or else punished for not resisting it. This answer assumes that aesthetic experience has a cognitive power achieved through reason and its deductions from a moral fable. Reason, supposedly, could discern universal order and direct the will toward virtuous action.

The seventeenth century also traced the pleasures of tragedy to the dramatist's skill in imitation, to the artistry of his language, to the Lucretian "return upon ourselves"—that is, to the excitement of witnessing others' misfortunes while we are secure in the knowledge that we do not share their danger—and to moral or otherwise stimulating emotions. Pity, it was thought, makes the audience compassionate, while fear combats pride. Moreover, excitement was valued for its own sake, as relieving a disagreeable indolence or mental vacuity. All of these seventeenth-century hypotheses continued into the eighteenth century.[1]

All of them appear in the critical works of John Dennis. But Dennis also drew on that intense commingling of large objects and mind-stretching passion termed "the sublime" to create a new model for making the disagreeables agreeable. Dennis, to be sure, called it "enthusiasm" rather than sublimity and found it in the epic rather than in tragedy. The heights of enthusiasm were too exclusively religious for anything as secular as tragedy to reach. Nevertheless, to transmute the terrors of the epic into something more pleasant, Dennis counted on enthusiasm in much the same way as Hazlitt and Keats would rely on the sublime to make tragedy agreeable.

The word *sublime* as used in the eighteenth century describes such emotions as awe, reverence, admiration, astonishment, and terror. It also describes the causes of these emotions in both art and nature. The sublime did not become well known in England until after 1674, when Boileau published his translation of Longinus's *Peri Hupsous* under the title *Traité du sublime, ou du Merveilleux dans le dis-*

cours. Before the late seventeenth century English critics had applied the word *sublime* only to a grand or lofty style. Thus the eloquence of the Bible, of biblical paraphrases, or of poems borrowing their style from the Bible was, on occasion, termed sublime, and this religious context linked the sublime with mysterious pleasures beyond those of imitation.[2] Also, qualities which after 1674 came to be called sublime were being discovered in nature. Marjorie Nicolson has shown that the concept of the "natural sublime," as distinguished from the Longinian or "rhetorical sublime," emerged in the seventeenth century before there was a name for it. The telescope had revealed a universe no longer limited in time and space and no longer earth-centered, as the Middle Ages had seen it, but lacking form, center, and perceptible plan. This new kind of universe, however, was quickly identified with the Deity and, indeed, seen as evidence of His infinite power. Newton's *Principia* defined infinite space as the "sensorium of God" and offered proof that order, proportion, and regularity are universal principles. In a world from which Locke had removed innate ideas, the mysterious emotions aroused by such ordered vastness were a welcome assurance that God existed. The next step toward an aesthetic of the sublime was to admire large objects as also producing feelings of immensity, expansion, reverence, and awe. Thus emotions once reserved for the Deity were transferred first to interstellar space, and then to large terrestrial objects, especially mountains, and finally to "objects" which, although not sizable, had physical or moral powers similar in their effects to magnitude.[3]

Peri Hupsous, through Boileau's translation, provided a name for these objects and for the overpowering feelings they aroused. It also affirmed the use of *sublime* to describe a mysteriously moving eloquence. For Longinus the sublime is the power in literature that elevates and transports the soul. This power resides in the energetic effects of an author's genius and imagination. Boileau's subtitle is a key to those energetic effects that distinguished the sublime in England. The *merveilleux* was soon found to lodge not only in the astonishing qualities of literature but also in mountains, oceans, vast armies, the heavens, and other great masses or spaces. Longinus had designated large bodies of water, the stars and the planets, and erupting volcanoes as "great" and "more divine" than lesser phenomena, but he does not endow these large objects with sublimity. The enjoyment of this greatness, rather, is evidence of man's capacity for elevated thoughts, that is, of his susceptibility to the sublime in literature.[4] The "natural sublime," more than Longinus's literary sublime, was responsible for the importance of size to sublimity.

As used in this study, the term "natural sublime" describes objects and effects found in nature or their emotional equivalent in other objects. Although originally shaped by writers who made it a religious experience, the natural sublime came to include other than pious emotions. Belief in an ordered universe did not preclude delight in its apparent irregularities and perils. The dangers of precipices and jagged rocks, fierce storms, beasts of prey, and eventually haunted castles combined terror with a pleasure that, with some ingenuity, might be rationalized as religious but was clearly enjoyed for its own sake. Similarly, although the mind-stretching so often attributed to the sublime might be regarded piously, it was also appreciated as releasing the mind from hateful or boring restraints. This mind-stretching could lay claim to only limited ratiocination and often dwindled into mere empathy with vastness. Certain rational assumptions—like that of an orderly universe—contributed to the history of the natural sublime, and, as we find in Dennis, the sublime might be valued for stimulating the reason to more penetrating insights; but the sublime might also be seen as putting reason aside. This separation of the sublime and the rational is important to the history of the sublime and the tragic.

The tragic and the sublime clearly share certain qualities. Sublime objects were often regarded as causing terror which, like terror in tragedy, may be rendered agreeable by its very intensity. Furthermore, characters in tragedy could become sublime by displaying qualities such as courage, fortitude, and magnanimity that duplicate the awe-inspiring effects of great size; and the style of tragedy was often thought sufficiently elevated to qualify for sublimity. On the other hand, some differences stood in the way of merging the sublime and the tragic. There are four principal differences, all of which proceed more from the natural sublime than from the Longinian sublime. They all imply the measurement of the sublime by the dimensions of time and space. Although in the eighteenth century the word *sublime* achieved a range of meaning including almost any sort of intense emotion and the causes thereof, it continued very often to reveal its bulky origins. One obvious difference between the sublime and the tragic is that a sublime derived from external nature could be more readily seen in paintings and in descriptions of large objects or great vistas than in men and women acting on the stage. James Thomson's *The Seasons* (1726–30), with its pleasing visible terrors but with no tragic confrontation of evil, was unmistakably sublime.[5] Samuel Johnson found sublimity in Milton's "awful scenes"; whereas, praising Shakespeare as the poet of human rather than external nature, Johnson distinguished Shakespeare's tragedies as "pathetick" rather than sublime.[6] Lord Kames, in his *Elements of Criticism* (1762), regarded the sublime "as applicable to every sort of literary performance intended for amusement"; but his illustrations, although sometimes drawn from Shakespeare's tragedies, mainly describe large or powerful objects. Although Kames readily admits figurative or moral magnitude to the sublime, he finds this sort of elevation most striking when it is displayed against the visual sweep of vastness, that is, as it appears in Milton. The "tender passions," he writes, are more peculiarly the province of tragedy; grand and heroic actions, of epic poetry.[7]

A second and closely related difference is the separation of the pathetic from the sublime in a somewhat different sense from Johnson's. For Johnson both the terror of the sublime and the tenderness of the "pathetick" were emotions shared by the reader or the audience. For Addison the sublime did not include the sharing of violent emotions. On this point Addison differed from Dennis, who had protested Longinus's admission that sublimity can exist without passion. Probably influenced by Addison, John Baillie decided in his *Essay on the Sublime* (1747) that the agitation of terror or any other passion destroys the "solemn *Sedateness*" which he found in the sublimity of large natural objects.[8] For Baillie, therefore, tragedy could not be sublime—not at least if the audience shared in feelings of pity and fear. The pathetic—that is, the sharing of the characters' emotions—had long been considered essential to the moral impact of tragedy. As an explanation of tragic pleasure, what Eric Rothstein calls the "affective hypothesis" was current in the late seventeenth and early eighteenth centuries. This hypothesis—evident in Rapin, Dryden, and Dennis—supposes that the emotions excited by tragedy are themselves moral agents.[9] Fear is supposed to subdue pride, and pity to instill mercy. Addison and Baillie found other moral values in sublimity, but their force did not reside in unsettling emotions.

A third difference between the tragic and the sublime lies in the religious bent of the latter, which turned it away from the theater, even the tragic one. Tragedy, Dennis admitted, is admirable as an instrument of moral instruction, but the very quality that makes it broadly useful limits its spiritual reach. Since it appeals only to the less visionary, it does not offer the inspiration needed for religious insight. For this quality, Dennis turned to the epic. The alliance between epic poetry and religion had been a long-standing one; preternatural creatures—early settlers in the epic population—had found homes that now looked very much like Alpine crags and wastes. *Paradise Lost*, which became the example of sublimity most frequently cited during the eighteenth century, offered biblically mythic figures against vastness stretching off into infinity. Even in the next century—as seen in Wordsworth, Coleridge, and De Quincey—the highest flights of sublimity were often confined to the Bible and Milton.

A fourth difference between the sublime and the tragic

6

—at least as the tragic was usually defined in the seventeenth and early eighteenth centuries—is that whereas tragedy appealed to both reason and emotion in order to make some rather precise ethical points, the natural sublime began and persisted as an emotional force, religious in impact to be sure, but often not in any very specific sense an instrument of religious or moral instruction. Addison, although he did not believe that tragedy should demonstrate poetic justice by rewarding innocence and punishing vice, insisted on an instructively moral fable. If, for Dennis, tragedy was not sufficiently emotional for the sublime, for Addison sublimity was too exclusively emotional for tragedy. Dennis believed that reason has far-reaching powers, including supersensory insight, and that enthusiasm, by stimulating reason to disclose God's benevolence, puts the world's torments and terrors in a reassuring light. In his essays on "Pleasures of the Imagination" (*Spectator* nos. 411–21) Addison, too, described the natural sublime—or "greatness"—as raising religious devotion to the "highest pitch"; but he denied greatness a partnership with reason.[10] Like Dennis, he found sublimity in the epic, but he reversed Dennis by making tragedy the superior genre (*Spectator* 39, 40). Although he thought of tragedy as basically religious, he apparently saw no reason to identify the religious intensity of greatness with tragedy's more specific moral inferences and feelings. Francis Hutcheson evidently agreed: he found the "grandeur" described in *Spectator* 412 something different from the moral beauty which, he thought, characterized tragedy.[11]

These four differences did not stand in the way of Edmund Burke, who in his *Philosophical Enquiry into the Origins of Our Ideas of the Sublime and Beautiful* (1757) identified the sublime with the tragic. If not to everyone's satisfaction, at least to the satisfaction of many of those who wrote on tragedy during the remainder of the century, Burke resolved the differences listed above. Big objects, craggy shapes, and vast spaces still provided the ultimate test of sublimity; Burke simply found their emotional equivalent in tragedy. This was not different from their emotional effect

7

in actual life, for the imagination, as Burke defined it, was only a substitute for sensation. It did not distinguish art from actuality. As for identifying the pathetic and the sublime, Burke took up where Dennis left off, thereby reuniting what Addison and Baillie had put asunder. According to Burke, the audience is wrung by terror but enjoys it. Although, like others, Burke based his sublime on religious assumptions, in tragedy he gave it a moral rather than a religious impact. But if he fitted the sublime to tragedy by giving it a moral thrust, he fitted tragedy to the sublime by making its effects entirely extra-rational or, indeed, counter-rational. Burke's sublime was still the sublime of time and space: a sensory response to the phenomenal world plus emotion untrammeled by thought. His fusion of the tragic and the sublime did more violence to tragedy than it did to the prevailing views of sublimity. In excluding the rational from tragedy, Burke offered a perversion of the tragic that was to dominate the criticism of tragedy for the rest of the century.

On the other hand, Burke's emphasis on emotion opened the definition of tragic pleasure to a rational dimension not dependent on a moral fable. As strong excitement gained ground as the important ingredient in tragedy, plot was depreciated until what was valued most was not a closely knit sequence of events leading to a moral conclusion but a series of moments with emotional impact and moral force. The need for sympathetic identification made character more important than action. Burke's identification of the sublime and the tragic pushed the criticism of tragedy in these directions. The result, although often sentimental and even foolish, was not altogether regrettable. The affective hypothesis as advanced by Burke acknowledged a roomier prescription for tragic structure than either Dennis or Addison would have allowed; and if the emphasis on emotion oversimplified tragedy, it eventually encouraged the exploration of tragic complexities.

To restore the intellectual dimension to tragedy, Dennis's model for dealing with the disagreeables had to be rebuilt. Even in 1704, when Dennis published *The Grounds of*

Criticism in Poetry, his model was already a bit old-fashioned, for it had some Neoplatonic parts which the new empiricism of Hobbes and Locke was about to replace. By 1712 the new empiricism as seen in Addison's essays on "Pleasures of the Imagination" had pretty well confined aesthetic pleasure to visual images recalled and combined by a picture-making faculty called the imagination. This faculty could provide considerable enjoyment, ranging all the way from mere recognition to sublime awe, and it could submerge in pleasing emotion even ugly bits of scenery; but, when it came to knowing such important truths as the dispensation of good and evil, it had to give way to judgment and reason.

It is on this stripped-down framework that Dennis's model had to be rebuilt to combine once again the intensity of the sublime with the powers of reason. It had to do no less than show how tragedy brings order into a world of ugliness and pain. The sublime simply could not do this as long as its reach was measured by external objects or even by their infinite extension. To evaporate the disagreeables, the sublime had to get the better of time and space: it had to become the sublime of vision and not merely the sublime of the visible. The measure of sublimity had to be the full scope of the human mind with all its resources.

Alexander Gerard in his *Essay on Taste*, published in 1759 only two years after Burke's *Enquiry*, followed Burke in identifying the sublime with the pathetic and therefore with feelings of terror. He gave the imagination a variety of powers beyond those allowed by Burke, including the power to make art something different in its effects from actual life; but his pleasures of the imagination, like Addison's, were still subintellectual. The pleasure that sublimity can bring to tragedy remained circumscribed by time and space. Richard Payne Knight in his *Analytical Inquiry into the Principles of Taste* (1805) offered a still more sophisticated analysis of the imagination. He recognized the power of imagination to bring more thought into the act of creation than either Addison or Gerard allowed, but once the sublime idea has been created, Knight clamps it down with the old restrictions of the visible sublime. Its effects become purely emotional ones, although, to be sure, Knight differs from Burke in believing that the sublimity of tragedy lies in sharing, not pity and terror, but the energy which the tragic character displays in either his violent or his tender actions.

It was not until Archibald Alison in his *Essays on the Nature and Principles of Taste* (1790) found sublime pleasure in the imaginative process itself, rather than in any equivalent to physical magnitude that it may create, that the sublime acquired rational insights. Knight, writing fifteen years later, had apparently read the *Essays* without comprehending the whole force of Alison's discovery. Alison marks the transition from the visible sublime to the visionary sublime. He left no doubt that the sublime derives its power from what goes on in the mind or that the magnitude accounting for this power is psychological and internal, not physical and external. By definition, Alison's sublime is a repudiation of the time-space world, even though the imagination must find its materials within the empirical framework of Hobbes and Locke. The imagination gains its power over the measurements of time and space as trains of associated ideas fuse imagery with both thought and feeling. These trains supply a kind of knowledge or truth superior to that expressed in the abstractions necessary to deductive reasoning. All human perception requires a selection of particulars from an undifferentiated mass of phenomena, and to that extent, as Hazlitt said, all ideas are abstract; but Locke's abstract ideas require a further degree of abstraction—for instance, the removal of particulars to free the idea of "a man" from the peculiarities of any individual man. These abstract ideas and the abstract language based on them have obvious uses, but their truth is different from and—as most Romantic poets and critics agreed—inferior to the kind of truth riding in Alison's trains, that is, to the dynamic truth of human experience that can reside only in the interaction of the particular and the general.[12] This complex of thought, feeling, and emotion, although prompted by sensory particulars, does not otherwise defer to spatial and temporal dimensions. It is uniquely a creation of the human mind. Since Alison had made the size and quality of the mental operation more important to sublimity than the size and quality of any external object, he could the more readily identify the sublime and the tragic; but his explanation of tragedy nevertheless turns out to be a disappointing one. It remained for Hazlitt, Shelley, Keats, and others to evaporate the disagreeable with the power to know as well as the power to feel, as sublime intensity makes thought more penetrating in its fusion with sensation and emotion.

The identification of the sublime with the tragic and its consummation in this view of tragedy will be traced from Dennis to Hazlitt and Keats through Addison, Burke, Gerard, Alison, and Knight. Other writers, as will be noted, shared in this process, but in these eight the main steps are evident. Dennis, Alison, Hazlitt, and Keats may be said to represent the sublime of vision, while Addison, Burke, Gerard, and Knight represent the sublime of the visible. To emphasize this grouping, I considered transposing the positions of Alison and Knight; but since in some respects Knight is closer to Hazlitt than Alison is, I decided to keep these chapters in chronological order. The chapters on Hazlitt and Keats are introduced by a short introductory chapter on "The Sublime of Vision" mentioning briefly, with no attempt at thoroughness, the sublime in Blake, Coleridge, Wordsworth, De Quincey, Shelley, and Hunt.

CHAPTER ONE

DENNIS

John Dennis came face to face with the natural sublime when he traveled over the Alps in 1688. "We walk'd," he wrote in a letter dated 25 October of that year, "upon the very brink, in a litteral sense, of Destruction; one Stumble, and both Life and Carcass had been at once destroy'd. The sense of all this produc'd different motions in me, *viz* a delightful Horrour, a terrible Joy, and at the same time, that I was infinitely pleas'd, I trembled." He contrasts the "transporting Pleasures" excited by these "vast, but horrid, hideous, ghastly Ruins" with the less intense delight in orderly landscapes that is more clearly "consistent with reason." Offering Thomas Burnet's explanation that the deluge had collapsed the shell of a once smooth and beautiful world, Dennis writes that "if these Mountains were not a Creation, but form'd by universal Destruction, . . . then are these Ruines of the old World the greatest wonders of the New" (2:380-81).[1] Dennis usually called these transports "Enthusiasm" or "Enthusiastick Passion" rather than "the sublime," reserving the latter term for speaking of Longinus. Dennis also encountered enthusiasm in literature: the classics, the Bible, and notably

13

Paradise Lost. Here again, as in the Alps, he found sublime passion in the "amazing effects" of "Divine Displeasure"; in fact, the comprehension of frightening irregularities as part of divine order is more astonishing than the irregularities themselves (1:201, 268-69).[2] This partnership of enthusiastic passion and reason distinguishes Dennis's treatment of the sublime. Reason increases passion, and passion stimulates reason to deeper insights. The imagination, with its vivid—and generally visual—images, is indispensable to this partnership if it is to attain enthusiastic heights.

1

In *The Advancement and Reformation of Modern Poetry* (1701) Dennis asserts that passion is "the chief Thing in Poetry" (1:215), but, as far as poetry is concerned, there is little evidence that he thought of even "Enthusiastick Passion" as ever setting reason aside. For Dennis, passion, memory, imagination, and reason were distinct faculties. As Dennis explains in *The Grounds of Criticism in Poetry* (1704), the memory retains images of objects no longer present to the senses. To produce "Works of Invention" the imagination selects and combines these images, possibly arriving at a new creation altogether. In the process of invention the imagination is stimulated by emotion and guided by "judgment" or "reason" (2:362–63). Reason is a logical and analytical faculty which, through its power of "understanding," preserves the distinction between "the Images, and the Things themselves," a distinction lost "in Fevers and Madmen" (1:218). But it is more than that. Despite the Hobbesian framework suggested by his analysis of invention, Dennis did not narrow reason as Hobbes had narrowed it and as it would generally be limited later in the century. For Dennis, reason is far from comprising only induction and deduction; it also employs empirical wisdom, revelation, authority, and even supersensory insight. Man's "aspiring Thoughts . . . are able to pass the Bounds that circumscribe the Universe" (1:202).[3] Reason, thus broadly conceived, is the faculty that

14

organizes all the faculties to perceive universal order, and so directs the will toward conformity with that order, i.e., toward virtue. It discovers "Rule and Order" in nature, and demands similar organization in art (1:96, 202–203).

But passion is equally necessary if poetry is to achieve both its "subordinate" and its "final" ends, which are, respectively, "to please" and "to reform the Minds of Men" (1:335–38). Dennis classifies the passions as "ordinary," or "vulgar," and "enthusiastick." In *Advancement and Reformation* he distinguishes "ordinary" passion as that "whose Cause is clearly comprehended by him who feels it," whereas the cause of enthusiastic passions "is not clearly comprehended by him who feels them" (1:216). In *Grounds of Criticism* Dennis adds that the "vulgar" passions, of which all men are capable, are moved by objects or ideas encountered in the "ordinary Course of Life." For example, "Anger is moved by an Affront; . . . Pity by the Sight of a mournful Object," etc. On the other hand, enthusiasm requires a mental operation of which "thousands are not capable" (1:338–40). Enthusiastic passions are moved not merely by mountains, precipices, or other natural objects but by "Ideas in Contemplation," wherein the idea of an object has been expanded by "thought." The expanding process is attended by that emotion which generally accompanies "Thoughts in Meditation" and which, when it becomes "strong," is enthusiasm. These large ideas produce "the same Passions that Objects of those Ideas would raise in us, if they were set before us in the same light that those Ideas give us of them." The conditional clause is important. There are no phenomena in nature that, without an attendant mental process involving both reason and passion, can produce enthusiasm. The idea exciting enthusiasm is never simply the visual representation of some external object. Enthusiasm becomes strongest when "rais'd by religious Ideas." Dennis illustrates the process of mental expansion, as well as its consummation in a religious idea, by his well-known example of the sun, which "in ordinary Conversation, gives the Idea of a round flat shining Body, of about two foot diameter," but which "occurring to us in Meditation, gives the Idea of a vast and glorious Body, and the top of all visible Creation, and the brightest material image of the Divinity." His second illustration is especially appropriate to the pleasures of tragedy: the idea of thunder "occurring in Meditation, sets before us . . . the most dreadful Phaenomenon in Nature," moving "a great deal of Terror in us, and 'tis this sort of Terror that I call Enthusiasm" (1:338–40). As this example suggests, Dennis finds the strongest enthusiasm in the natural sublime, with, of course, a strong biblical contribution to the expansive process of thought. In analyzing the ideas responsible for enthusiastic passions, he first cites God, the angels, and "other Creatures of the immaterial World," then "Heavenly bodies . . . and the Immensity of the Universe," and finally large terrestrial objects: "Seas, Rivers, Mountains" (1:345, 347, 348, 350). Although we can equate "enthusiasm" to "sublimity," Dennis does not give us any terms to distinguish between the "sublime" and the "beautiful" (except perhaps in a letter dated 1 Oct. 1717, where he writes of "the *pulchrum* as well as the *dulce* in Poetry" [2:401]). *All* good poems—whether marked by enthusiastic or vulgar passions—must be "beautiful," i.e., regular, ordered, and reasonable. The *sublime* (or *enthusiastic*) *beautiful* seems superior to the *nonsublime beautiful* mainly in its religious force. Although, says Dennis, only the "strongest" enthusiastic passions are religious in origin (1:339), his analysis of enthusiasm always stresses a religious or at least a wonderful cause (1:216, 356, 361).[4]

Dennis is not very explicit, psychologically, in describing the expansive process of meditation; but, although he does not use the word *imagination* in this particular context, his description of imagination elsewhere would seem to apply. That is, under the direction of reason and accompanied by increasing emotion, the imagination selects and combines images that have been stored in the memory. Enthusiastic passions make a special demand on the imagination. Most affecting are images of sight and hearing; and especially conducive to enthusiasm is a terrible object pictured—as Homer and Virgil can picture it—"in violent Action or Motion" (1:362–63). Visually precise images propel the imagination beyond the immediately visible (1:105), and Milton's "crouding" of images as he describes the Creation both raises admiration and satisfies the reason (1:277).[5] These two latter points bring Dennis close to Alison and Hazlitt, who explained the energetic effects of clear particulars and of massed images in terms of association. But it would be incautious not to qualify Monk's remark "that in this, the earliest theory of the sublime in England, the author turns to association to explain aesthetic experience" (p. 49). One can only agree that association, in a general sense of the word, seems to have been at work. At least this explanation is consistent with the Hobbesian scheme, suggested by Dennis's description of invention, of the "swift succession of one thought to another" accelerated by passion and directed by judgment.[6] However, a precise explanation in terms of the empirical psychology seems out of the question, since Dennis, essentially more of a Neoplatonist than a Hobbesian, is not relying only on sensory data as a source of knowledge (1:188, 202).[7] What is clear is that the efficient cause of enthusiastic passion is an idea imaginatively forming and finally formed inside the mind, so that at last it bears but little resemblance to the external object that prompted its formation. Although this idea implies the vast realm and power of God as its final cause, the size of the initiating object is less important to Dennis than the idea itself, the expansive process of forming it, and the mental capacity necessary to its formation.

Admiration is the principal enthusiastic passion. The others are terror, horror, joy, sadness, and desire. Chief among these—and the only one besides admiration that Dennis treats in detail—is terror. The place of terror—or, indeed any shared emotion—in the sublime was a disputed point. Dennis takes Longinus to task for admitting the possibility of sublimity without passion, but, he adds, Longinus's description of the sublime implies that passion is always aroused (1:359–60).[8] John Baillie found the "agitation" of the passions at odds with the sublime: a generalization that may

17

reflect his experience as a physician with the British Army as well as the influence of Addison. An intense passion shared by the viewer or reader, he says, destroys the "one simple, grand *Sensation*" and the accompanying "solemn *Sedateness*" necessary to the sublime.[9] In identifying the sublime and the pathetic Dennis anticipates Edmund Burke and Alexander Gerard, who in 1757 and 1759, respectively, made terror part of sublime pleasure. Baillie, like Addison, focuses his analysis of sublimity on external objects and their magnitude; but, Dennis, as always, is more interested in what goes on in the mind. Terror, which Dennis introduced into the sublime, reaches its height only after considerable "meditation."[10] "Fear . . . or Terror, is a Disturbance of Mind proceeding from an Apprehension of an approaching Evil, threatning Destruction or very great Trouble either to us or ours. And when the Disturbance comes suddenly with surprize, let us call it Terror; when gradually, Fear." The causes of "common Terror" are "things . . . powerful, and likely to hurt," whereas the causes of "Enthusiastick Terror" are the "Ideas of those Objects." Religious ideas cause the greatest terror, for what can be more terrible "than the Idea of an angry God?" (1:356, 363). Other causes of enthusiastic terror include ideas of "Serpents, Lions, Tygers, Fire, War, Pestilence, Famine, &c." (1:361), but of course these are still ideas expanded in meditation to go beyond "common life" and to suggest, at least, a link with the divine. The object that in common life would have caused "noxious" feelings has merged in a large, elevating, and intensely pleasing idea (1:263, 264).

The *enjoyment* of great poetry requires the same sort of process as its creation, that is, the meditative or imaginative expansion of an idea (1:105, 110, 462; 2:222). Moved by an object brought within reach of sight and hearing, passion excites the reason to a kind of insight that acts as immediately as sensation itself (1:362–63). "In a sublime and accomplish'd Poem, the Reason, and Passions, and Senses are pleas'd at the same Time superlatively." This joint operation not only intensifies the pleasure of each faculty—sharpening, for instance, the reason's perception of the poem's moral and its orderly design—but satisfies "the whole Man together" (1:263–64).

2

What Dennis says about enthusiasm and enthusiastic terror does not apply explicitly to tragedy, for in tragedy the "vulgar" passions predominate. In *Grounds of Criticism* Dennis divides poetry into two classes according to the "greatness" of the passion, or, in other words, according to its power to please and instruct: (1) "the greater Poetry . . . [which] comprehends Epick, Tragick, and the greater Lyrick Poetry," and (2) "the less Poetry . . . [which] includes . . . Comedy and Satire, and the little Ode, and Elegiack and Pastoral Poems." Greater Poetry is further subdivided according to the prevalence of enthusiastic or vulgar passions. The former prevail "in those parts of Epick Poetry, where the Poet speaks himself, or the eldest of the Muses for him, . . . [and] in the greater Ode." The vulgar passions, on the other hand, "prevail in those parts of an Epick and Dramatick Poem, where the Poet introduces Persons holding Conversation together." This category includes tragedy, of course. Perhaps this is the reason, Dennis conjectures, why Aristotle preferred tragedy to the epic, that is, because its prevalent vulgar passions enable it to "please and instruct more generally" (1:338–39). The epic is more pleasing and instructive for those who can form the ideas necessary to enthusiastic passions, but tragedy is more pleasing and instructive for the less talented majority. Dennis proposes to "treat of the Vulgar Passions when we come to speak of Tragedy" (1:339), but the *Grounds of Criticism* ends without this part having been reached.

When Dennis does deal specifically with tragedy as in *The Usefulness of the Stage* (his reply to Collier in 1698), he relies on reason to control—and thus render pleasurable —those passions that would otherwise be unpleasant. Strong passions are "transporting" but only within an orderly scheme perceptible to reason. Thus the moral, religious, and political effects on which Dennis centers *The Usefulness of the Stage* are "naturally pleasing." Noble and virtuous passions are stimulated by moving examples, while those passions "whose Excesses cause their Vices" are modified by the distribution of rewards and punishments (1:153, 164).[11] Among his illustrations Dennis includes a political version of the Lucretian return: "People who are melted or terrified with the Sufferings of the Great . . . are rather apt to feel a secret Pleasure" that their more docile citizenship frees them "from the like Calamities" (1:165).

With its emphasis on reason's power over the passions, this is a rather conventional account of tragic pleasure. In the *Grounds of Criticism*, where Dennis is dealing with the epic rather than with tragedy, he is more original, although he still cites some of the usual reasons why the disagreeables can become pleasant. "Those very Passions which plague and torment us in Life, please us, nay, transport us in Poetry" when reason has subjected them to "the exact perpetual Observance of Decorums" (1:264). Thus Dennis is among those who believe that the poet's artistry surmounts the disagreeable. He also resorts to the Lucretian return. After he has attributed enthusiastic terror to the fear of God, it seems a bit anticlimactic for him to add: "no Passion is attended with greater Joy than Enthusiastick Terror, which proceeds from our reflecting that we are out of danger at the very time that we see it before us" (1:361). Or, again, to take comfort in fictitiousness: "For, tho' sometimes a vigorous lively Imitation of Creatures that are in their Natures noxious, may be capable of giving us Terror, yet Nature, by giving us a secret Intelligence that the Object is not real, can turn even that tormenting Passion to Pleasure" (1:264). But as shown by the words "reflecting" and "Nature," this is all part of "meditation," with its component of reason acting immediately to provide an awareness of truth. What we are out of danger from is not the truth symbolized by the idea (of God or his powers) but some actual external object, such as a tiger or lion, which has been assimilated by meditation into a symbol

of order. The reader whom great poetry restores "to Paradise
. . . beholds . . . [Tygers and Lions] with Joy, because . . .
[like the first man] he sees them without Danger" (1:264–65).
Of course, as many passages testify, Dennis does not exempt
this later Adam from the fear of God. God "may deliver us
from all other Terrors, but nothing can save and defend us
from him" (1:362). Just as in *The Usefulness of the Stage*
Dennis fits the suffering of tragic characters into a harmonious pattern of divine or civil dispensation deducible from
the action, so in *Grounds of Criticism* he fits the lions and
tigers into an idea of God intuited through meditation. If
Dennis seems to offer some usual explanations of pleasure
arising from unpleasant materials—that is, the artistry of the
imitation, the Lucretian return, and the awareness of fiction
—he has made all of these an integral part of his aesthetic.
The pleasure does not reside in security from objects which
in actual life would cause pain and suffering, but in the perception of an idea—of God or His attributes—arrived at by
a rather complex process which was initiated by the noxious
object and in which the noxious object now appears as part
of God's plan. This process, with its interplay of emotion
and reason, has harmonized all the faculties in an enjoyable
—and immediate—hyperawareness of order both in the poem
and in Providence.

If in *Grounds of Criticism* Dennis had got around to the
vulgar "Compassion and Terror" of tragedy, he could—and
one may guess that he would—have used this distinction between objects and ideas to account for the pleasures arising
from ordinarily unpleasant materials. Vulgar passions, like
enthusiastic ones, are also moved by "Thoughts" or "Ideas."
When, in order to define "enthusiasm," Dennis compares the
effect of an object in "ordinary conversation" with the effect
of an idea expanded in meditation, he is not—despite his use
of the word "ordinary"—distinguishing between "vulgar"
passions and "enthusiastick" ones. Even the vulgar passions
may arise from "Thoughts in Meditation" (1:216–17, 338–
39).[12] Therefore Dennis could have dissolved the disagreeables in tragedy by the same means he used to deal with the

disagreeables in the epic. Tragic characters and their actions, expanded by meditation, would invite terror, but this expansion would involve reason, thereby providing an immediate comprehension of God's justice. This comprehension would be enforced, undoubtedly, by deductions from a moral fable.

Dennis was a forerunner in advancing strong excitement as an explanation of tragic pleasure, anticipating Du Bos and Fontenelle, who have been considered influential in introducing this theory into English criticism, and also, of course, Burke.[13] But a firm rational element distinguishes him within the strong-excitement school. According to Eric Rothstein, Dennis was among those whose interest in strong excitement opened the way to emotional, or "sentimental," tragedy. The seventeenth-century acceptance of emotional excitation as an important source of pleasure, Rothstein argues, encouraged the sentimental tragedy of the eighteenth century. Moments of excitement came to be more highly regarded than the "ramified totality" of a moral fable. Even Dennis, between *The Impartial Critick* (1693) and *The Usefulness of the Stage* (1698), reveals this shift in emphasis.[14] In the former, when "Compassion and Terrour" leave the audience "serene again, and . . . less apt to be mov'd at the common Accidents of Life, after it has seen the deplorable Calamities of Hero's and Sovereign Princes," its serenity is due to deduction rather than sympathy (1:33); whereas in 1698 Dennis speaks of hearts being softened by "moving Compassion" (1:164). Nevertheless, even on the same page in *The Usefulness of the Stage* and in passages already cited in *Advancement and Reformation* (1701) and *Grounds of Criticism* (1704), it is clear that Dennis does not exempt reason from controlling both the artistic and the moral order in poetry. According to Du Bos, the mental activity caused by strong excitement is in itself so pleasurable that men will indulge their passions even when they know that the consequences will be painful.[15] But Dennis, except perhaps in his Alpine report, does not represent passion as enjoyable unless it is moderated by reason. The kind of strong excitement that Dennis values brings *all* the faculties into play.

3

In several respects Dennis occupied a position well advanced toward the explanation of tragic pleasure found in Hazlitt and Keats. It would be difficult, of course, to show a direct influence, and this analysis does not argue for one.[16] During the years between Dennis and Hazlitt, the empirical psychology brought about a systematic explanation of aesthetic pleasure and an analysis of the imagination in terms of association. Dennis had not been that precise, and, besides, he was not essentially an empiricist. Also, according to Dennis, tragedy discloses a providential order which is morally compelling; whereas Hazlitt and Keats find order within the tragic character himself rather than in divine supervision. But in his treatment of "enthusiasm" Dennis makes several points also found in Hazlitt and Keats: the exciting effects of clear particulars, individually and in mass; the pleasure and harmonious self-realization of the various faculties working together; the interaction and mutual dependence of the faculties in the creation and enjoyment of great poetry; and, especially, the importance of intense emotion in stimulating the reason and thus converting the disagreeables through an intuition of truth.

Since Dennis thought of enthusiastic emotions as more religious than those excited by dramatic poetry, he did not identify sublime pleasure and tragic pleasure, but he drew on sublime or enthusiastic pleasures to make the disagreeables disappear much as Hazlitt and Keats would do it for tragedy. For Dennis the efficient cause of sublime emotion is not an object outside the mind or its emotional equivalent but an idea formed in meditation. Physical size is not important in the efficient cause, although infinite space remains an attribute of the final cause. What counts more than the size of the initiating object is the sizable process of thought leading to ideas of God and his powers. This aggregating process is important for the mutual stimulation of reason and passion; and as the sublime idea is attained, the various faculties are also brought together in a perceptive and satisfying harmony. Thus, although it may initiate such a process, an unpleasant object cannot, in itself, be the cause of sublime emotion. The cause is, rather, the process of fusing thought and feeling with the initial impression in order to create an idea or symbol. Evil is no longer seen as it would appear outside the aesthetic experience. It is not dismissed as unreal or distant but presented as part of a higher and truer reality, or—in Dennis's terms—part of "reason" and "nature." It retains its power to excite intense emotion: indeed, in the translating process, this power is heightened. Thus, although his psychology cannot be equated with that of empiricists like Alison and Hazlitt, Dennis led the way toward an explanation of tragic pleasure which, eventually made in terms of this psychology, infused the tragic with sublime feeling and profound knowing.

CHAPTER TWO

ADDISON

Unlike Dennis, Addison deals with the pleasures of the imagination as distinct—or almost distinct—from those of other faculties. Addison's imagination is that empirical faculty which Hobbes dismisses as "nothing but decaying sense" or, in its combining role, as producing only "a fiction of the mind."[1] For Hobbes and Locke, imagination principally means the recall, or the recall and combination, of visual images. The combinations of "fancy," says Locke, "may give pleasure and delight"; but when it comes to "dry truth and real knowledge," the "figurative speeches" of fancy do "nothing else but . . . insinuate wrong ideas, move the passions, and thereby mislead the judgment; and so indeed are perfect cheats."[2] Addison tries to restore the imagination—or, as he sometimes calls it, the fancy—to respectability, but, like Hobbes and Locke, he keeps it clear of a penetrating awareness of truth. He has not attempted to restore Dennis's partnership between reason and imagination.

Dennis and Addison both turn to the natural sublime for emotions useful in converting the disagreeables. For Dennis, the sublime evaporates the disagreeables by means of an expansive psychological process, promoted by emotion and controlled by reason, that results in a state of religious insight termed "enthusiasm." For Addison, the sublime also offers a religious experience; but, since Addison's imagination relies mainly on visual data with little help from any form of reason, sublime passion is not accompanied by any very complete idea of providential order. Large objects can also force the mind to stretch itself out of "Sloth and Idleness." In Addison, as in others after him, the pleasures of the sublime hesitate between these two poles: an elevated but not precise or complete sort of knowing and an expansive kind of mental exercise enjoyable for its own sake. This ambiguity could not be resolved to handle the disagreeables in tragedy until the pleasurable mind-stretching became a means of knowing some sort of moral order. In Addison, as in most other eighteenth-century writers on the sublime, it had not achieved this added dimension. The disagreeables that sublimity can render pleasant did not yet include the omnipresence of evil.

1

Although other senses may contribute to aesthetic pleasure, Addison's "Pleasures of the Imagination" (*Spectator* 411–21) are dominated by images of sight, which is "the most perfect and most delightful of all our senses."[3] The "Primary Pleasures . . . entirely proceed from such Objects as are before our Eyes," whereas the "Secondary Pleasures . . . flow from the Ideas of visible Objects, when the Objects are not actually before the Eye, but are called up into our Memories, or form'd into agreeable Visions of Things that are either Absent or Fictitious" (*S.* 411). Here Addison is distinguishing not between the effects of objects and of ideas, as his phrasing might suggest, but between the effect of ideas formed from objects "before our Eyes" and the effect of ideas formed from "Absent or Fictitious" things. In each case the immediate cause of pleasure is an *idea*. Addison follows Locke in defining "light and Colours [as] only ideas in the Mind, and not qualities . . . in Matter."[4] The mind may further contribute to a pleasing idea by adding, through association, not only enriched visual delights, but the pleasures of other senses and even religious feeling. Despite these additions, the pleasures of the imagination remain distinguishable by qualities commonly ascribed to visible objects.

Primary pleasures "all proceed from the Sight of what is *Great, Uncommon,* or *Beautiful*" (*S.* 412).[5] Addison defines the *uncommon* less clearly than the other two kinds of pleasure: it offers agreeable surprises, gratifies our curiosity, and provides new ideas. The *beautiful* resides in the opposite sex, in gay and varied colors, in symmetry and proportion, and in ordered variety. It "gives a Finishing to any thing that is Great or Uncommon" (*S.* 412). The *great* has the qualities of the natural sublime. Like Dennis, Addison rejected the Longinian word *sublime* when describing the effects of natural objects. Apparently he preferred the term "greatness" because it avoided the rhetorical implications of Longinus's sublime.[6] In his papers on *Paradise Lost* Addison had already used "greatness," although not consistently, to distinguish magnitude of action and theme from sublimity of thought and style (*S.* 267, 279, 285, 333). Now, perhaps, he also wanted to separate his own conception of sublimity from Dennis's "enthusiasm" and some of its suggestions. "Greatness" proves to be less agitating than "enthusiasm," for Addison agreed with Longinus that the sublime is not always "mixt and work'd up with Passion" (*S.* 339). Moreover, Addison may have distrusted "enthusiasm" as overemphasizing the sensuous in poetry and, despite Dennis's case for its partnership with reason, as suggesting irrationality in religion.[7] But Addison is like Dennis in turning to his own travels in the Alps, to natural philosophy, and to the Christian religion for the topography of greatness and its spiritual implications.[8]

> By *Greatness,* . . . [Addison does] not only mean the Bulk of any single Object, but the Largeness of a whole View, considered as one entire Piece. Such are the Prospects of an open Champian Country, a vast uncultivated Desart, of huge Heaps of Mountains, high Rocks and Precipices, or

27

a wide Expanse of Waters, where we are not struck with the Novelty or Beauty of the Sight, but with that rude kind of Magnificence which appears in many of these stupendous Works of Nature. Our Imagination loves to be filled with an Object, or to graspe at any thing that is too big for its Capacity. We are flung into a pleasing Astonishment at such unbounded Views, and feel a delightful Stillness and Amazement in the Soul at the Apprehension of them. The Mind of Man naturally hates every thing that looks like a Restraint upon it, and is apt to fancy it self under a sort of Confinement, when the Sight is pent up in a narrow Compass, and shortned on every side by the Neighbourhood of Walls or Mountains. On the contrary, a spacious Horison is an Image of Liberty, where the Eye has Room to range abroad, to expatiate at large on the Immensity of its Views, and to lose it self amidst the Variety of Objects that offer themselves to its Observation. Such wide and undetermined Prospects are as pleasing to the Fancy, as the Speculations of Eternity or Infinitude are to the Understanding. (*S.* 412)

The perception of objects in some great mass or pattern expands the mind by extending the imagination to the limits of its capacity. In *Spectator* 412 this expansion seems to be entirely visual: the "Sight" ranges widely without being able to grasp the whole vast panorama. In no. 413, however, association adds an idea of God and therefore a dimension of thought to the mind's expansion.

It is because they are essentially religious that Addison, like Dennis, gives a high place to the pleasures of sublimity. Addison is not sure of the immediate causes of the pleasures of the imagination, since within the empirical limits he has set for himself we do not know the "Nature of an Idea, . . . the Substance of a Human Soul," nor the "Conformity or Disagreeableness of the one to the other" (*S.* 413). He does not, like Akenside in *The Pleasures of Imagination* (1744), lay aside epistemological caution to describe greatness, novelty, and beauty as emanations of "the mind supreme."[9] Nevertheless, Addison believes that the final cause of the pleasures of the imagination may lie in "the Goodness and Wisdom of the first Contriver." That the *uncommon* should be enjoyable is consonant with God's encouraging men to form new ideas; and pleasurable *beauty* shows God's benevolent interest in multiplying the population and, through his gift of light and color to the imagination, in rendering "the whole Creation more gay and delightful." The *great* brings man closest to an idea of God and therefore provides the most pleasure. Created to enjoy the contemplation of his Creator, man naturally delights

> in the Apprehension of what is Great or Unlimited. Our Admiration, which is a very pleasing Motion of the Mind, immediately rises at the Consideration of any Object that takes up a great deal of room in the Fancy, and, by consequence, will improve into the highest pitch of Astonishment and Devotion when we contemplate his Nature, that is neither circumscribed by Time nor Place, nor to be comprehended by the largest Capacity of a Created Being. (*S.* 413)

The Deity, having already been identified with the infinite, is now identified with the large object, which thereby becomes a source of religious pleasure.

God's "Nature" as suggested by a sizable object is clearly infinite vastness; and as far as the pleasures of the imagination are concerned, there is no reason to think that it needs to be anything else. There are, of course, other possibilities, depending on how much the viewer's mind is allowed to become involved. The sublime expansion would not have to be purely visual. For instance, to the moment of observation the mind might bring a store of analogies which could be finally exhausted without giving the viewer a full comprehension of the extent, causes, or effects of the vast assemblage before him. Or the mind might use inductive reasoning to arrive at the idea of God which Locke describes in a passage quoted in *Spectator* 531.

> The complex *Ideas* we have both of God, and separate Spirits, are made up of the simple *Ideas* we receive from *Reflection*; v.g. having from what we experiment in our selves, got the *Ideas* of Existence and Duration; of Knowledge and Power; of Pleasure and Happiness; and of several other Qualities

and Powers, . . .: When we would frame an *Idea* the most suitable we can to the supreme Being, we enlarge every one of these with our *Idea* of Infinity; and so putting them together, make our complex *Idea of God*.[10]

Or the mind might draw on its knowledge of the Scriptures. Locke's complex idea of God, says Addison, fails to show us God "in all the Wonders of his Mercy." If we are to know God "not only as infinitely Great and Glorious, but as Infinitely Good and Just in his Dispensations toward Man," we must have "Recourse to Revelation" (*S.* 531). The mind might even apply its knowledge of God's goodness and justice to problems of good and evil. Thus a thoughtful and inquiring mind could gather its resources to form an idea of God and his dispensation that would be very complex indeed. But thoughtful inquiry is not exactly the state of mind for which Addison contrived the pleasures of the imagination.

These pleasures require very little of the understanding. "It is the whole Soul," Addison writes in *Spectator* 600, "that remembers, understands, wills, or imagines"; but in *Spectator* 411–21 Addison is very far from allowing the imagination to activate the whole soul. The pleasures of the imagination, while "not so gross as those of Sense," are not "so refined as those of the Understanding" (*S.* 411).[11] As a comparing, distinguishing, and abstracting faculty—in this capacity sometimes called "Judgment"—the understanding determines the poet's choice of language and accounts for the pleasures of comparing an imitation with the original (*S.* 416, 418); but otherwise it does not obtrude. One of the attractions of the pleasures of the imagination is the absence of hard thought. "Easie," "gently exercising," "conducive to Health," these pleasures awaken the faculties from "Sloth and Idleness, without putting them upon any Labour or Difficulty." Theirs is not the "Bent of Thought . . . necessary to our more serious Employments" (*S.* 411). Yet a serious bent of thought is precisely what Addison considered necessary to religious assent. He followed Locke and Descartes in seeking a "bond between intellect and belief."[12] Since this bond depends largely on deductive reasoning,[13] the pleasures of the imagination do nothing to establish it; nor, indeed, when it comes to religious knowledge, "Astonishment and Devotion" do no more than reassure the viewer of large objects that the Deity is present. Presumably the viewer has recognized that the emotions aroused by limitless space are much like those excited by Christian supernaturalism.

But the enjoyment of religious mystery does not account for all the pleasures which Addison ascribes to greatness. All these pleasures may be termed religious in the sense that they are due to God's complaisance, but as the mind grasps at something "too big for its capacity," it enjoys the process of escape in addition to any idea of God which may be recalled (*S.* 412). Addison agrees with Du Bos, Fontenelle, and others in his time that indolence and languor, "Sloth and Idleness," are the enemies of pleasure (*S.* 411). He would dispel these states of mind with a moderate degree of excitement. It is almost as if Addison and others who attribute to sublimity the dual pleasure of contemplating infinitude and escaping sloth subscribe to the latter pleasure because they feel the intellectual shortcomings of the former. In any case, for a hundred years or so, both kinds of pleasure were ill-assorted partners in sublimity. The mind's delight in freedom to explore some vast space and the resulting feeling of accomplishment in overcoming difficulty remained an important part of the sublime experience. Others, including Baillie and Gerard, also describe this kind of delight in terms suggesting an analogy with physical freedom and exertion. Hume makes this analogy explicit: "Now 'tis certain, that the tendency of bodies, continually operating upon our senses, must produce, from custom, a like tendency in the fancy . . . as if our ideas acquir'd a kind of gravity from their objects." Whereas Addison—and, like him, Baillie and Gerard—emphasize the mind's projection over an extended object or area, Hume describes the difficulties of surmounting height and of traversing past time. As the imagination climbs from successive part to part to reach some height or—without the help of such resting places—attempts the even more difficult task of pushing back against time in order to grasp the idea of a re-

mote object, the mind rejoices in its sense of difficulty overcome and is even incited to seek further triumphs of the same
sort.[14] Thus the exploring, surmounting mind is compared
to an exploring, surmounting body. Critics persisted in describing the process of mind-stretching as a kind of empathy,
physical as well as mental. Lord Kames describes not only the
"capacious and aspiring" mind but also the whole body striv-
ing to match the large object: "A great object makes the
spectator endeavor to enlarge his bulk. . . . An elevated
object . . . makes the spectator stretch upward, and stand
a-tiptoe."[15] Keats, as he looked at the Ambleside falls in 1818,
"never forgot [his] stature so completely."[16]

Addison, like others after him, attributes these expansive
powers not only to actually large objects, but to objects with
equivalent emotional effects. He grants that architecture
may possess not only "Greatness [in] the Bulk and Body of
the Structure," but also in "the Manner in which it is built."
He cites the Tower of Babel, the pyramids, and the Wall of
China among examples of the former and "one of Lysippus's
statues of Alexander" and the Pantheon at Rome—as distinguished from the much larger "Gothick Cathedral"—as examples of the latter. Grandeur of manner makes use of bold and
rounded forms, which allow the eye to "surround" a body
and so grasp its wholeness more fully (*S.* 415). Addison may
also be suggesting that Lysippus's statue of Alexander owes
its "Majestick Air" not only to a capability of being visually
surrounded but to association with Alexander's heroic qualities. This sort of moral size may add pleasure, perhaps, but
visual magnitude remains the final test of Addison's idea of
greatness.

2

Addison makes a parallel analysis of the secondary pleasures of the imagination, paying more attention, however, to
the psychological process of association and less to the analogy
with freedom to roam at large. The secondary pleasures arise
not from objects "actually before our Eyes," as primary

pleasures do, but "from Objects . . . that once entered in at
our Eyes, and are afterwards called up into the Mind, either
barely by its own Operations, or on occasion of something
without us, as Statues or Descriptions." To enjoy this pleasure we need not have seen the actual objects that are imitated
but only something resembling them. For "the Imagination,
when it is once Stocked with particular Ideas" can "enlarge,
compound, and vary them at her own Pleasure." These secondary pleasures proceed, principally it seems in *Spectator*
416, from comparing "the Ideas arising from the Original
Objects, with the Ideas we receive from the Statue, Picture,
Description, or Sound [of the language] that represents them."
Addison follows Aristotle in detailing the pleasures of imitation (*Poetics* 4). We are pleased to discover likenesses and
differences between the representation and the original and
also by the mental activity required in this process, although,
Addison grants, this comparing and abstracting might "more
properly [be] called the Pleasure of the Understanding" (*S.*
416, 418). But in other essays the pleasures of the secondary
imagination are not so limited. The pleasures excited by
great poetry are the same three kinds as primary pleasures,
and apparently not inferior to them. Homer, Virgil, and
Ovid represent, respectively, the great, the beautiful, and the
strange. "Reading the *Iliad*"—in contrast to the "well-
ordered Garden" of the *Aeneid* and Ovid's "Scene of "Mag-
ick"—"is like travelling through a Country uninhabited,
where the Fancy is entertained with a thousand Savage *Prospects* of *vast Desarts*, wide *uncultivated* Marshes, huge For-
ests, mis-shapen *Rocks* and Precipices." Having added that
Homer's characters "are most of them God-like and Terrible," Addison concludes—with his first use of the word *sublime* in this sequence of essays— that "*Homer* fills his Readers
with Sublime *Ideas*" (*S.* 417). The words that I have italicized
in Addison's description of the *Iliad* also appear in his description of greatness as a source of primary pleasures (*S.* 412),
and, in addition, *a Country uninhabited, mis-shapen rocks,
and precipices*, and *marshes* recall, respectively, the following
features in the earlier description: *open* or *unbounded*

Views, huge heaps, and *Expanse of Waters.* Greatness in poetry, obviously, duplicates the pleasurable effects of greatness
in nature, and does this by "striking the Imagination" as
smartly as external objects do (*S.* 417).[17] In fact the pleasures
of poetry may surpass primary pleasures in intensity. A poet
can "get the better of nature" by adding "more vigorous
Touches" to a landscape. Thus the poet "heightens its
Beauty, and so enlivens the whole Piece, that Images, which
flow from the Objects themselves, appear weak and faint, in
Comparison of those that come from the Expressions." A
"warm Fancy" is needed to supply the images and a "discerning Judgment" to select expressions with a generally forceful
impact. The artist produces, through association, "a more
complex Idea" than the subject itself can excite (*S.* 416). The
artist's imagery gives increasing pleasure as it initiates trains
of ideas drawing on a rich pattern of association. For the
greatest enjoyment, both a "noble Writer" and his perceptive
reader should have their minds stored with images appropriate to various kinds of poetry (*S.* 416, 417).

In this description of the associating process that intensifies the secondary pleasures, we find one of Addison's approaches to the disagreeables. Addison offers a "Cartesian"
explanation: ideas from a "Prospect or Garden, having entered the Mind at the same time," remain there in "a Sett of
Traces belonging to them in the Brain, bordering very near
upon one another"; when one of these ideas is recalled, it
"dispatches a flow of Animal Spirits to its proper Trace,"
exciting all the ideas not only in that particular trace, but also
in the adjoining traces of the set, until "the whole Prospect
or Garden flourishes in the Imagination." This reactivated
prospect is not exactly like the original, however, because a
dominant feeling of pleasure aroused by some pleasant recol-
lection will widen the "Passage worn in the Pleasure Traces"
while it narrows and quickly stops up those traces that belonged to "disagreeable Ideas" from the original impression.
This pleasure "overcomes" any "little Disagreeableness' (*S.*
417).[18] Like Hartley's theory of vibrations in the "white
medullary substance of the brain,"[19] Addison's Cartesian

"traces" with their animal spirits are a curiosity in the history of the imagination. But in neither case does the discredited physiology invalidate the associating process Addison and Hartley try to explain: not only the capability of an image to set off a train of related ideas but the power of a dominant feeling to direct and unify the ideas in such a train.

By "little Disagreeableness" Addison means only objects that blemish a landscape. In handling bigger disagreeables he is conventional. Comparing an imitation with the original is one source of pleasure, even when the object lacks greatness, novelty, or beauty. A second source of pleasure is the emotion we share with the characters: it is easy to understand why we enjoy sharing emotions like hope, joy, and love, but the pleasures of terror arise more "properly" from "the Reflection we make on our selves" when confronted by terrible objects or suffering characters. Once more the Lucretian return: "When we look on such hideous Objects, we are not a little pleased to think that we are in no Danger of them." And "when we read of Torments, Wounds, Deaths, and the like dismal Accidents, our Pleasure does not flow so properly from the Grief which such melancholy Descriptions give us, as from the secret Comparison which we make between our selves and the Person who suffers"—although, as a further condition to our enjoyment, we must be aware that the suffering is "past" or "fictitious." As with Dennis, the painful object has been modified by "reflection" as it becomes part of a pleasure-giving idea; for Dennis, however, terror has not been diminished into self-congratulation, but moved up to a higher level of divine administration—a level knowable only to intellectual powers which Addison keeps apart from the imagination. Dennis's lions and tigers, although temporarily amiable in Eden, have been assimilated into the idea of a terrible God, whose terrible aspects are increased rather than diminished by the assimilation. But, says Addison, "we look upon the Terrors of a Description, with the same Curiosity and Satisfaction that we survey a dead Monster" (*S.* 418). God, to be sure, created the monster; but dead, the monster is not going to hurt anybody, whereas the animals in Eden become predatory after the fall.

Addison found his illustration of "greatness" in the epic, not in tragedy. He thought highly of tragedy, calling "a perfect Tragedy . . . the Noblest Production of Human Nature" (*S.* 39); and probably he considered the pleasures of tragedy too complex to be included among the "easie" pleasures of the imagination. In his essays on tragedy, which antedate his essays on the pleasures of the imagination by well over a year, one would not expect him to have discussed "greatness"; but this is no reason why he could not have mentioned tragedy in *Spectator* 411–21 if he had thought it appropriate to do so. Addison does cite "Sublimity of Expression" as desirable in tragedy (*S.* 42), but there is nothing to suggest that this includes the pleasure that he would later attribute to "greatness." More likely "Sublimity" refers, as it frequently does in Addison's papers on *Paradise Lost,* to elevated thought and style. The papers on tragedy (*S.* 39, 40, 42, and 44) deal rather conventionally with the pleasures of this genre. Addison has something to say about artistry in constructing plots (he opposes tragicomedy and double plotting) and touches on the appropriateness of style, sentiments, dress, decorations, and stage effects; but he traces the audience's chief delight to moral and religious improvement. Tragedy can give "the Mind one of the most delightful and most improving Entertainments" by representing "a Virtuous Man . . . struling with Misfortunes. . . . Diversions of this kind wear out of our Thoughts every thing that is mean and little. They . . . cultivate . . . [our] Humanity, . . . soften Insolence, sooth Affliction, and subdue the Mind to the Dispensations of Providence" (*S.* 39). Since "Terrour and Commiseration" are necessary to produce this "pleasing Anguish in the Mind," the audience must not feel confident that virtuous characters will be suitably rewarded at the end of the play. Addison, therefore, provoked an attack from Dennis by repudiating poetic justice in tragedy. "We find that Good and Evil happen alike to all Men on this Side the Grave; and as the principal Design of Tragedy is to raise Commiseration and

Terrour in the Minds of the Audience, we shall defeat this great End, if we always make Virtue and Innocence happy and successful" (*S.* 40.)[20] But, although he denied that rewards or punishments should be dealt out according to innocence or guilt, Addison did not reject a moral fable. The most important quality of the fable, in fact, is its moral. No pity or admiration is appropriate for characters who suffer in an evil cause (*S.* 39).[21] Evil must not be presented in a sympathetic light, and, to this extent, the providential distinction between good and bad must be deducible from the action. There is nothing strikingly original in these reasons why tragedy pleases: the dramatist's artistry, the encouragement of moral emotions and the discouragement of immoral ones, admirable characters resisting or enduring evil, and reconciliation with Providence. But these pleasures require a degree of reasoning that Addison did not associate with the pleasures of greatness. Tragedy and greatness both encourage piety; but, as we have seen, the religious experience that greatness provides is incomplete. Greatness might be said to resolve the disagreeables—if the rude aspects of sublimity may be considered such—into a pleasing (if rudimentary) idea of God and also into some expansive mental exercise pleasant for its own sake. These rude aspects appear not only in actual large objects but in their emotional counterparts suggested by the *Iliad.* But greatness, although it offers some feeling of God's infinitude, tells us nothing of his role in dispensing good and evil. For this additional knowledge Addison's pleasures of the imagination would have to be supplemented by reason.

3

Addison's "greatness" shares certain qualities possessed by Dennis's large or enthusiasm-exciting ideas. In the first place, for both Dennis and Addison, expansive astonishment rises immediately from an idea in the mind of the viewer or reader. In the second place, the final cause of these pleasures is religious, the natural sublime involving an identification of large objects with the Deity. Both Dennis and Addison find the greatest pleasure in the contemplation of God. Finally, in this contemplation of the Divine, the rude or rough aspects of sublimity become pleasant. But there are differences. For one thing, Addison's greatness is less exciting than Dennis's enthusiasm; it does not agitate us with terror. More importantly, within the aesthetic experience Addison does not bring the imagination and the mind's intellectual powers into partnership. Reason, or the faculty needed to demonstrate truth, is left out. "Greatness" provides twin thrusts of primary pleasure: (1) the contemplation of God offered by large objects and (2) the exhilarating experience of stretching the mind. The ability of greatness to deal with the disagreeables is limited to a pleasant but inchoate kind of knowing and to the mental stimulation of a vicarious journey in space.

When it comes to the secondary pleasures, Addison opens up a further way of handling the disagreeables: trains of associated ideas may be so dominated by a ruling passion that the disagreeables evaporate within the complex idea built up by the trains. This is a kind of mind-stretching, too (although Addison does not confine it to greatness), with a potential for extending the trains of association to bring the whole "soul" to bear on the problems of good and evil. But Addison limits the trains to an interplay of imagery and emotion, involving a modicum of judgment but not requiring full intellectual power. The "Disagreeableness" that is overcome is truly "little."

Addison stops well short of giving the imagination the highest truth-finding power or the pleasure commensurate with such power. He stops short of the harmony of energy and insight that Dennis achieved through the extra-empirical faculty of reason and which Hazlitt and Keats, benefiting from a long line of empirical philosophers and aestheticians, were to achieve through the empirical faculty of the imagination. But Addison at least projected the powers of the imagination toward creating beauty from the frequent ugliness of truth.

CHAPTER THREE

BURKE

Its implications of physical size and religious insight readily identified the sublime with the epic and with descriptive poetry. Less than half of the eighteenth century had passed, however, before the sublime frequently came to mean heightened emotion of any sort. Early in the century, intense sympathy began to outweigh reasoned deduction as important to tragedy; and since sublimity could mean merely the "intensely moving," tragedy could more readily be called "sublime." In his translation of Longinus (1739), William Smith looks forward to Burke, but without forsaking Addison and Baillie, when he describes the storm scenes in *King Lear* as sublime in their addition of "solemnity to terror."[1] But sublimity in a more precise sense was still often kept distinct from tragedy, as it had been by Dennis.

1

Edmund Burke in his *Philosophical Enquiry into the Origin of Our Ideas of the Sublime and Beautiful* (1757) was the first to use the terrors of the sublime to explain the pleasures of tragedy in systematic detail.[2] For Burke, the terror evoked by tragedy is an intense and shared emotion, different from the "solemn sedateness" of Baillie or the "delightful stillness" of Addison. It is closer, in sheer emotional force, to Dennis's enthusiasm, but without any component of reason. Evil is known only by our physical and emotional reaction to it, which gives the audience a moral push, to be sure, but which lacks anything like the religious insight stimulated by enthusiasm.

Burke designates two principles—*"self-preservation* and *society"*—as responsible for most of the powerful impressions that ideas can make on the mind. The first explains the sublime; the second, beauty. The sublime arises from any threat to life or well-being, that is, from "whatever is fitted in any sort to excite the ideas of pain, and danger, that is to say, whatever is in any sort terrible, or is conversant about terrible objects, or operates in a manner analogous to terror, . . . that is, . . . [whatever produces] the strongest emotion which the mind is capable of feeling" (pp. 38–39 [pt. 1, secs. 6, 7]). The efficient causes of sublimity, therefore, include fear, obscurity, power, privation, vastness, infinity, succession and uniformity, magnitude, difficulty, magnificence, powerful or flashing lights, dark and gloomy colors, excessive or sudden or uncertain sounds, angry cries of wild beasts, bitter smells and tastes, and feelings of pain (pp. 57–87 [2. 1–22]). When the resulting pain becomes too great or too imminent, the effect is only terrible; but "the feeling which results from the ceasing or diminution of pain" is often agreeable. Burke calls "this species of relative pleasure . . . *Delight"* (pp. 34–36 [1. 3–4]). On the other hand, the less intense pleasures of beauty stem from our enjoyment of "society," that is, our "sense of affection and tenderness" toward other creatures. Anything—such as a small, smooth, gradually varied, delicate, or mildly colored object—that induces this sense is therefore an efficient cause of beauty (pp. 40–42, 51, 113–17 [1. 8–10, 18; 3. 13–18]).

The imagination contributes to these pleasures only by supplying the equivalent of sensation. In the *Reflections on*

40

the Revolution in France (1790) Burke objects that man's "naked reason . . . lacks the wardrobe of a moral imagination, which the heart owns and the understanding ratifies." "Prejudice" (a continuing sense of rightness) and "prescription" (title based on ancient and unqualified possession) are strongholds of reason clothed with moral imagination.[3] Here imagination has the power to incorporate reason in symbols for moral and political guidance, but in the *Enquiry*, which Burke drafted as early as 1747, the imagination represents "at pleasure the images of things in the order in which they were received by the senses," or combines "those images in a new manner, and according to a different order." This "sort of creative power . . . is incapable of producing anything absolutely new." In arousing the passions, the imagination is "only the representative of the senses, . . . [and] can only be pleased or displeased with the images from the same principle on which the sense is pleased or displeased with realities" (pp. 16–17 ["Introduction on Taste"]).

Burke minimizes the mental activity required by his sublime pleasures. These pleasures, in fact, are inimical to thought. Fear "robs the mind" of its power to reason. The sublime reaches its "highest degree" in "astonishment," or "that state of the soul, in which all its motions are suspended, with some degree of horror. In this case the mind is so filled with its object, that it cannot entertain any other, nor by consequence reason on that object which employs it" (p. 57 [2. 1]). The most mind-shaking ideas reach into the obscurity of the infinite, precluding any understanding. "A clear idea is . . . another name for a little idea" (p. 63 [2. 4]). In accounting for our sublime pleasures Burke even questions the power of association: "when we go but one step beyond the immediately sensible qualities of things, we go out of our depth" (pp. 129–30 [4. 1]). Burke looks, instead, to "the natural properties of things" for an explanation of the pleasures of the sublime and the beautiful. Noting that pain and fear exhibit like physical symptoms, he concludes that "pain and fear consist in an unnatural tension of the nerves." Beauty, on the other hand, "acts by relaxing the solids of the whole system," producing "an inward sense of melting and languor" (p. 149 [4. 19]).

Association, Burke grants, may help create the *idea* of danger, but it will not account for the *pleasure* resulting from such an idea (p. 134 [4. 5]). Although association helps expand an object to sublime size or its emotional equivalent, the pleasure comes—not from the process of expansion—but from the impact of the now-expanded object on the nerves. The only difference between pain and terror is that the causes of pain "operate on the mind, by the intervention of the body," while the causes of "terror generally affect the bodily organs by the operation of the mind suggesting danger" (p. 132 [4. 3]). That is, both the *sensation plus association* that gives rise to terror and the *pure sensation* that gives rise to pain provide exactly the same kind of nervous tension and the same kind of delight. Any sort of ratiocination has been removed from the immediate cause of sublime pleasure. To evaporate the disagreeables Burke turns, therefore, to the familiar abhorrence of lassitude and the analogy of physical exercise. The mind needs exercise to keep its parts "in proper order" (p. 135 [4. 6]). Terror provides this sort of exercise, and if it is "so modified as not to be actually noxious" by threatening immediate destruction, the result is delightful (p. 136 [4. 7]). Burke traces this delightful "tension or contraction" of the muscles to each of his categories of sublime objects. Large visual objects, for instance, cause a delightful degree of pain either because "all the light reflected from a large body should strike the eye in one instant" with a vast number of rays or because "the eye must traverse the vast space of such bodies with great quickness, and consequently the fine nerves and muscles destined to the motion of that part must be very much strained" (p. 135, p. 137 [3. 6, 8]). It is one of Burke's strengths in the *Enquiry* that he bases his argument firmly on the "sensible qualities of things"; nevertheless, his physiological explanation of fear invited criticism and ridicule, Richard Payne Knight pointing out, for instance, that one's pen a foot away makes a greater impression on the retina than Salisbury steeple at a mile, and that the sheet of paper on which one writes would be more sublime than the Peak of Teneriffe.[4] Burke's emphasis on the physiology of the sublime does little to dignify the pleasures of tragedy.

2

Since Burke was only making a philosophical inquiry into the origin of our ideas on the sublime and the beautiful, we ought not expect him to offer a complete theory of tragedy. Nevertheless, in view of his exclusion of reason from the aesthetic experience and his limitations on the powers of association, it is difficult to see how his pleasures of tragedy could have included more than certain physiological responses and their moral thrust.

These pleasures stem from both *"self-preservation* and *society"*—that is, from both the sublime and the beautiful, with the power of terror to tighten up and the power of pity to relax our nerves. This nervous activity pleases because it is our nature, as designed by the Creator, to protect ourselves from danger and to feel affection for others. An "inconsistency" in this reasoning was cited in 1812 by the Reverend Basil Richard Barrett, who makes sympathy the chief source of tragic pleasure but does not agree that terror itself is pleasurable. Terror, says Barrett, is no more pleasant than grief, and just as grief must be "absorpt by [the] superior pleasures [of] social affection," terror must be overcome by "curiosity" —a palliative that had been advanced by numerous other followers of Burke who, like Barrett, rejected terror as enjoyable.[5] Burke, of course, acknowledges that terror becomes pleasant only when by not "pressing too close" it provides the thrill of danger without any immediate threat to safety. The pleasures of tragedy are both self-regarding and benevolent. "We have a degree of delight, and that no small one, in the real misfortunes and pains of others," and we also take pleasure in sympathizing with those in distress. Yet these feelings, while satisfying a natural propensity in ourselves, have a moral force. They are "blended with no small uneasiness, which prompts us to relieve ourselves by relieving those who suffer; and all this antecedent to any reasoning, by an instinct that works to its own purpose, without our concurrence" (pp. 38, 45–46 [4. 6, 14]). The point that tragedy pleases through a moral sympathy with "merit and worth" had been made at least as early as Shaftesbury, but Burke gave it a new force and influence.[6]

Burke's stipulation that danger must not "press too close" does not imply a difference in kind between the pleasures and tragedy and those provided by actual misfortunes. Imitation, to be sure, adds an increment of pleasure to the former; but our pleasure in imitation results principally, without any interaction of reason, from the social affections that prompt us to copy what others do (p. 49 [6. 16]).[7] Burke takes issue with the Addisonian variety of the Lucretian return, which holds that misfortune is more enjoyable if we realize its fictitiousness. "The nearer tragedy approaches reality, the more perfect its power." Burke then adds his famous illustration of the audience deserting "the most sublime and affecting tragedy" to witness the execution of "a state criminal of high rank" in the square adjoining the theater (p. 47 [1. 15]).[8] Enjoyable pain may even press very close (if not "too close"), for we delight in the sufferings of others even when our own lives are in danger, or pity others when our own sufferings are greater (p. 48 [1. 15]). Some degree of immunity from danger is only a condition, not a cause, of enjoyment.

3

Any knowledge of evil which the pleasures of tragedy include is compounded, obviously, of only sensation and emotion: a combination which pleases the audience and moves it toward moral action. Burke is always careful to exclude the operations of reason. One may rationally infer something of the role of evil in human life from *a study of the passions*, which will suggest that the Creator wisely made evil a force for good; but this is not an inference from tragedy itself.

For Burke, the disagreeables become agreeable by arousing passions which the Creator intended to be agreeable, directed as they are toward self-preservation and social affection. Basically these passions of terror and pity are enjoyable because they provide a pleasant tensing and relaxing of the nerves. This arrangement makes it possible to enjoy a share in the fear and pain of those who suffer, while it adds the also pleasurable impulse to relieve their suffering. In stimulating feelings of pity and terror, imagination remains but a substitute for sensation—and sometimes an inferior one. Association aids the imagination in building up an idea to arouse the passions, but otherwise it cannot account for the pleasure with which the idea strikes the nerves. The pleasures of nervous stimulation leave no room for thought.

As I have noted in the Introduction to this study, Burke represents a version of what Rothstein calls the "affective hypothesis" as distinguished from the "fabulist hypothesis." The fabulist hypothesis was given its clearest definition by Thomas Rymer in the 1670's. Rymer held that the action of a tragedy teaches the lesson of "poetical justice" and, in its pattern of cause and effect, reveals the working of the divine cause.[9] In its most rigid form poetic justice assumes unambiguous rules which the characters in tragedy, and the audience as well, may advantageously follow or catastrophically violate. On the other hand, the affective hypothesis turns the moral force of the play over to sympathetic emotions.[10] Burke advances this hypothesis by strengthening the power of emotion as a moral substitute for reason. The moral effect of terror, however, is different from that explained by Dennis and Dryden, who think of terror as controlling pride. Aside from vaguely suggesting the divine power latent in magnitude of one sort or another, Burke's terror seems to have only an indirect moral influence. That is, our delight in terror attracts us to scenes of misery, which, in turn, arouse our pity and prompt our benevolence (p. 46 [4. 14]). For Burke, the sublime is always pathetic; in this respect, as well as in its intensity, Burke's sublime matches Dennis's "enthusiasm." Sharing the tragic victim's terror, we feel the "no small uneasiness" that impels us to relieve the pain of others. With its strong feeling and with the vague sort of providential sanction it gives to anything it touches, the sublime fits very well into the affective hypothesis. Although theologically more dilute, this sort of providential sanction supplants the fable's demonstration of God's ways to man. Burke's moral effects do not call for a closely plotted fable. His doctrinal commitment to the action is very slight. A tragedy must arouse those feelings of self-preservation which the Creator has intended for our well being, but it does not have to demonstrate His concern to the audience. It need only show sympathetic characters suffering disaster.

4

Dennis, Rapin, and Dryden subscribed to both the fabulist and the affective hypotheses as mutually supporting, for the moral feelings of humility and compassion seemed to be in keeping with the dispensations of a just providence. But as time passed, critics followed Burke in assigning importance to the immediate emotional response rather than to the fable. Even when they call for a well-unified action, they are likely to rank it low among the reasons why tragedy pleases. Hugh Blair, while holding out for unity of action, echoes Burke in attributing tragic pleasure mainly to "the social passions," with the awareness of fiction, "the propriety of sentiment and language, and the beauty of action" in distinctly subordinate roles.[11] Lord Kames also likes a well-linked chain of events (*Elements of Criticism*, 1:408–409; 2:406), but he explains "the whole mystery [of why we seek out the tragic] by a single observation, That sympathy 'tho painful is attractive, and attaches us to an object in distress" (1:447–48, n.). Here there is at least some recognition that, with or without any theological import, a well-ordered sequence of events provides aesthetic pleasure. However, this recognition is too occasional and too subordinate to keep the affective hypothesis from making room in theory for some developments that, as early as Shakespeare, had already taken place in practice: the relaxing of extra-human controls, the transfer of greater interest from supernatural agency to individual human beings, and the resulting emphasis on character and de-emphasis of a closely ordered action. The affective hypothesis helped relieve tragedy—or, more precisely, the theory of tragedy—of the awkward burden of theological demonstration.

The pattern of divine dispensation with which Rymer had stiffened the fabulist hypothesis had long been discredited by the practice of the great writers of tragedy, even though, when the great English tragedies were being written, the poets themselves joined the critics in defending tragedy as showing God's justice consummated.[12] Greek, Elizabethan, and Jacobean tragedies do not testify that tragedy must assume any system, cosmic or otherwise, for exalting virtue and punishing vice. Shakespeare's love-crossing stars and puddering heavens give moral astronomy only a ragged design for Providence. As George Steiner writes, "when there is compensation, there is justice, not tragedy."[13] This has been the consensus of critics at least since the Romantic Period, but there remains a consensus that a tragedy must offer the audience some sort of reconciliation with the disastrous outcome. "Reconciliation" implies "rightness"—even "justice"—of some sort, for which criticism frequently looks beyond faithfulness to actual life or artistic congruence among the parts. Nietzsche, although dismissing the principle of poetic justice as "brash and shallow," finds that Aeschylus enthrones ultimate moral responsibility "above men and gods alike." This "transcendental concept of justice" does not save Prometheus from suffering for his "noble ambition," but such crimes as his and his punishment by the gods are the price man pays for the "highest good."[14] A. C. Bradley sees in Shakespeare's tragedies a "world travailing for perfection," where good overcomes evil but "only by self-torture and self-waste."[15] For this moral scheme Bradley turns back almost a century to Hegel, whose use of the terms "right," "justified," and "justice" Bradley nevertheless regrets as "all out of place in a discussion of tragedy."[16] In contrast to Greek tragedy, Hegel believes, modern tragedy shifts the interest from external moral demands to personality. Reconciliation may still be found in some sort of justice—if only political—but, compared with the eternal justice Hegel finds in Greek tragedy, it is "more akin to that of a criminal court" and leaves the need for additional reconciliation within the individual himself. This reconciliation may lie in his awareness of religious salvation, in his assertion of strength and freedom, in his acceptance of the punishment as merited, or—lacking any of these—only in the audience's recognition that the "spiritual nature" of the noble character calls for his destruction by the "external accidents of the world in which he lives."[17] Bradley, "re-stating" Hegel on reconciliation, describes "the catastrophe as the violent self-restitution of the divided spiritual unity."[18] Modern criticism has continued to look for reconciliation within the tragic character rather than in the dispensations of extrahuman authority.[19]

The tragic character's power to put his world in order provided Romantic criticism with its tragic resolution. Burke's concentration on sympathy, and hence on character, helped move criticism in this direction, although it overlooked any need for exploring a character's thought.

5

Of course, the stress on pure emotion went too far. If Burke tested tragedy by its approach to the horrors of actual life, some of his followers who joined him in extending the affective hypothesis wanted to soften tragedy and its horror. The early eighteenth century, Philip Hobsbaum has argued, was still so close to the Civil War that "the tragic ideal of personal martyrdom or monastic austerity was abandoned in favour of a middle-class asceticism that pervaded worldly affairs. After a busy life, the appropriate fate was not a tragic fall but a rural retirement."[20] Apparently this need for moral comfort persisted into the second half of the century. Burke's followers, unlike Burke himself, were inclined to elevate compassion above fear as a source of tragic pleasure. They looked uneasily on horror. Campbell, White, and Blair found scenes of horror destructive of pity, which they considered the chief pleasure of tragedy. According to Campbell, pity is not "a simple passion," but a group of closely associated passions. Pity includes all the emotions excited by tragedy: the first of these, *commiseration*, engages the second, *benevolence*, which in turn engages the third, *love*. Commiseration is painful; benevolence is partly painful and partly pleasant; while love always implies "one of the noblest and most exquisite pleasures whereof the soul is susceptible, and which is itself, in most cases, sufficient to give a counterpoise of pleasure to the whole."[21] Lord Kames allowed a category of "pathetic tragedy," which, as distinguished from "moral tragedy," has pity for its chief passion and calls for innocent, rather than mixed, characters to excite this feeling.[22] Anna Letitia Aikin (later Mrs. Barbauld) would also have limited the degree of terror in tragedy. Pleasurable pity depends on "misfortunes . . . not . . . too horrid and overwhelming." The mind should be "softened" rather than "stunned" or "shocked"—as it is by "the trampling out of Gloster's eyes." Because it avoids extremes of horror, "a well written novel generally draws more tears"—and is therefore more pleasing—"than a tragedy."[23] This preference for softening contributed, it seems, to the popularity of the ending Nahum Tate supplied for *King Lear* in 1681, an ending which—Arthur Murphy reported in 1756—"will always be most agreeable to an Audience, as the Circumstances of *Lear's* Restoration, and the virtuous *Edgar's* Alliance with the amiable *Cordelia*, must always call forth those gushing Tears, which are swelled and enobled by a virtuous Joy."[24] Murphy rules out Shakespeare's ending as too terrible for the audience's sensibility to bear. Presumably he does not rule out the deductions of reason as a source of pleasure, but mainly he values Tate's moral fable for its power to evoke comfortably sympathetic emotions.

But if Burke's emotionalism contributed to this increasingly sentimental view of tragedy, even to the melodramatic terrors of the Gothic,[25] and to a disregard of thoughtful content, it also encouraged a new approach to intellectual insight. According to the fabulist hypothesis, it is mainly deduction from the interplay of character and action that accounts for the "thought" of a tragedy. In the latter half of the eighteenth century and in the Romantic Period, Shakespearean criticism related the thought more fully to the powers of language. A tragedy, it became evident, was to be read as poetry and not, as Aikin believed, as a disappointing substitute for a novel. F. R. Leavis has said that even Samuel Johnson read Shakespeare as though he were a novelist.[26] But other critics show an increasing sensitivity to Shakespeare's language, recognizing in Shakespeare's ending of *Lear*, for instance, insights and values that are more satisfying both intellectually and emotionally than Tate's sentimentalism.[27] It was the new proclivity to discuss textual points—Hobsbaum believes—"that brought the most refined criticism." He cites the various interpretations of Albany's "Fall and cease" (5. 3. 263) as evidence that criticism was "approaching a recognition of the true complexity of Shakespearean verse" (pp. 502–503). This interest in the text and consequently in the richness of the verse cannot be traced only to Burke and the affective hypothesis; yet it is compatible with this hypothesis in making individual sensibility, rather than deduction from a fable, the key to understanding and appreciation.

In this way Burke may be linked, at some distance to be sure, with Hazlitt's and Coleridge's analyses of the language and images of Shakespeare's tragic poetry. Also Burke's concern for the emotional intensity of tragedy anticipates a similar emphasis in Hazlitt and Keats, although in Hazlitt and Keats this emphasis does not exclude reason. Furthermore, Hazlitt and Keats trace sublime emotions to sympathetic identification with character rather than to the logic of plot, and for emotional force both depend on the "immediately sensible qualities" of an object. Burke's insistence on the particular as the basis of truth is both a strength and a weakness. Burke steers away from the shoals of abstraction, but his imagination is merely a substitute for sense, with no power beyond collecting and combining impressions of the external world. The "idea" compounded by association gives pleasure through its impact on the nervous system and not through any operation of the mind. Therefore Burke must limit the effects of tragedy to sensation and to emotion rising from a tension of the nerves. His approach to tragedy offers no means of seeing how the tragic character or the tragic poet puts his world in order.

CHAPTER FOUR

GERARD

From Burke's *Enquiry* until the end of the century English criticism most frequently offered sympathy as the reason why tragedy pleases.[1] Yet, only two years after the *Enquiry*, Gerard set alternative courses for the imagination to attack the disagreeables. Gerard remains close to Burke in making terror a shared emotion—that is, he, too, identifies the sublime with the pathetic—but this feeling is to be judged pleasant or unpleasant as it is modified by other feelings aroused by a tragedy. A passion is to be defined not as representing certain classes of actual objects but in relation to that unique object which is the work of art itself. Yet Gerard has only partially freed sublimity from the domination of large objects and their mind-stretching effects. His account of tragic pleasure, although centered on the individual work with its conversion of the unpleasant into the pleasant, still draws on earlier accounts of the sublime for pleasures excited by physical size. Mental activity continues to be pleasing for its own sake rather than for the production of knowledge. To take care of the disagreeables Gerard has gone beyond Addison and Burke in enlarging the powers of the imagination, but he stops short of bringing all the resources of the mind into the creative process. As a result the aesthetic experience is defective in its intellectual and moral dimensions.

1

Alexander Gerard, a Scottish minister and professor of philosophy as well as divinity, is best known for his *Essay on Taste* (1759).[2] His *Essay on Genius* (1774), however, is a useful supplement to the earlier work. Although the *Essay on Taste* includes "eclectic borrowings not entirely reduced to order,"[3] it is—partly for that reason—helpful in showing the relation of the sublime to the tragic, as well as the status of the imagination, in the mid-eighteenth century. Taste, says Gerard, is the pleasant feeling excited by the imagination as it unites the responses of the various senses. The senses contributing to the pleasures of taste are, in addition to the usual five, seven "internal" or "reflex" senses: "the sense of novelty, of sublimity, of beauty, of imitation, of harmony, of ridicule, and of virtue."[4] These are called "senses" because their perceptions are immediate, involuntary, and, in effect, "simple" (pp. 144–49 [3. 1]). As in Francis Hutcheson, to whom Gerard acknowledges his debt, they are "internal" and "reflex" because what they perceive is not an object outside the mind but an idea or set of ideas compounded by the imagination (p. 260 [4. 5]).

The imagination or fancy is a combining and modifying faculty. To make its "simple" effect, it combines and modifies the ideas supplied not only by each internal sense but by *all* the internal senses.[5] Far from being "wild and lawless," it combines images according to certain "general rules, associating chiefly ideas of such objects as are connected by the simple relations of *resemblance, contrariety*, or *vicinity*; or . . . the more complex ties of *custom, co-existence, causation*, or *order*" (pp. 153–54 [3. 1]). These "laws" are "fixed" in human experience. Despite some variations in individual perception or experience, therefore, an object may be said to have a "natural and usual effect" based on "determinate and stable [qualities], independent of humour or caprice" (pp. 72; 212, 214 [1. 7; 4. 2]).[6]

Association connects ideas into trains. Within these trains the ideas communicate "their [emotional] qualities to one another" so that ideas that would be "disparate and separate" to the external senses appear to the internal senses united in "one image." This mutual modification of associated ideas is important, as we shall see later, in Gerard's resolution of the disagreeables. It enables the mind to "take in a long train of related ideas with no more labour than is requisite in viewing a single perception" (pp. 155–60 [3. 1]). This is a pleasant thing to do, says Gerard, and the pleasure, although remaining "simple" and immediate, increases with the length and complexity of trains. As practice matures the taste, the mind comes "to comprehend, to retain distinctly, and to compare with ease, the most complicated habitudes, and the largest and most intricate composition of ideas" (p. 109 [2. 5]). To account for all this pleasure, Gerard expresses the usual eighteenth-century aversion to "indolence and languor" and sees the pleasure of taste arising as the mind is "forced to exert its activity, and put forth its strength, in order to surmount any difficulty" (pp. 3–6 [1. 1]). The mind's response to concrete particulars is a pattern of association that becomes more and more enjoyable as the mind learns to organize more complex structures. Gerard anticipates Hazlitt when he finds the invention of genius marked by "a readiness to associate the remotest ideas that are in any way related" (p. 163 [3. 2]). A mature taste must be ready to respond with equal facility.

Alison and Hazlitt use wide-ranging association to provide the mind with reasoned conclusions as well as exercise, but Gerard does not go this far. Although the pleasures of taste may make the discoveries of the superior faculties more interesting or attractive, Gerard is hesitant about letting his range of internal senses penetrate very deeply into the organization of nature or human life. The pleasures of taste remain something distinct from—and inferior to—the higher pleasures of reason and the moral faculty.

As he describes each sense, Gerard emphasizes mind-stirring as pleasurable in itself. Novelty relieves indolence and languor by giving an "impulse to the mind" and "putting it in action" (p. 7 [1. 1]). Both beauty (of visual images) and harmony (of sounds) keep the mind active with the interplay of uniformity and variety (pp. 33, 57 [1. 3, 5]). Imitation and ridicule exert the mind in comparison and contrast (pp. 47, 62 [1. 4, 6]). Gerard ranks the internal senses according to the amount of mental exertion that each requires, but the highest pleasure arises when a work of art addresses itself to the largest number of senses and thereby involves the mind most completely (pp. 137, 266 [2. 7; 4. 5]).[7]

Sublimity is one of the most stirring internal senses. Its causes and effects show how much Gerard's aesthetic depends on qualities found in visual masses. In his section on "grandeur and sublimity" (where these two terms are synonymous), Gerard closely follows John Baillie. In his *Essay on the Sublime*, published posthumously in 1747, Baillie draws sublime emotion from the sight of large objects which, through their visual extension, extend the mind:

> . . . every Person upon seeing a grand Object is affected with something which as it were extends his very Being, and expands it to a kind of *Immensity*. . . . Hence arises that *Exaltation* and *Pride* which the Mind ever feels from the *Consciousness* of its own *Vastness*—That *Object* only can be justly called *Sublime*, which in some degree disposes the Mind to this *Enlargement* of itself, and gives her a lofty *Conception* of her own *Powers*. (P. 4)

Objects with this power include, of course, mountains, oceans, and the heavens. The soul exalts in expansion to and beyond the dimensions of such objects and in thus advancing toward "the *Perfections* of the *Universal Presence*" (pp. 5–6). Since familiarity may dull the effect of even such vast objects, the high degree of "admiration" that must always attend the sublime calls for "uncommonness" (pp. 11–12), but a more important quality is "uniformity" or "simplicity." Little parts "shuffled" into a scene divert the imagination as it tries to form "one large and *grand Idea*." If the large object is uniform as well as large, says Baillie, "there is to the Imagination no Limit of its Vastness, and the mind runs into *Infinity*, continually *creating* as it were from the *Pattern*" (p. 9). The imagination that "creates" the idea of vastness does so by combining the visual images actually before the eyes into a complex idea and then enlarging this idea with repetitions of the same visual pattern. Reflecting on its ability to visualize great extension, the mind acquires a splendid conception of its power. The mind has a better opinion of itself if it can reach "the vastest Sensation" easily without having to fret about a lot of distracting detail. This easy extension "composes" the mind to "a solemn *Sedateness*" (pp. 9–10).

Baillie says nothing about association extending the mind beyond this unified mass of images. He limits the role of association to bringing small objects or nonvisible causes—such as the passions—up to emotional size. The sublimity of these causes can be measured only by their effect on the observer. "Thus we judge of the *Courage* of a Person, by his Steddiness in braving *Dangers*; of his *Piety*, by the just Adoration he pays to the *supreme Being*." Provided with great moral dimensions by means of association, "the *Sublime* of the *Passions* must influence the *Mind* in the same manner as the *Sublime* of *natural Objects*." (pp. 16, 19). This is a matter not of sharing an agitating emotion—for Baillie believes that such agitation would destroy "solemn *Sedateness*" (pp. 9–10)—but of seeing some strong passion, through its vast effects, as equivalent to visible size. Sublimity in the arts and sciences likewise depends on association. In architecture association with "*Riches, Power*, and *Grandeur*" or with "*Strength* and *Durableness*" may make even a small building able to extend and elevate the soul, while in painting sublimity consists in representing either large objects or actions associated with sublime passions (pp. 35–37). Music and science reach the sublime through association with great passions or great extension (pp. 38–41), while "the *Sublime* in *Writing* is no more than a Description of the *Sublime* in *Nature*, and as it were painting to the *Imagination* what *Nature* herself offers to the *Senses*" (p. 3). Association contributes to sublimity only by duplicating the emotional effects of visible magnitude.

Gerard acknowledges his debt to Baillie (p. 11, n.). "Objects are sublime," he says, "which possess *quantity*, or amplitude, and simplicity in conjunction" (p. 11 [1. 2]).

> When a large object is presented, the mind expands itself to the extent of that object, and is filled with one grand sensation, which totally possessing it, composes it into a solemn sedateness, and strikes it with deep silent wonder and admiration: it finds such a difficulty in spreading itself to the dimensions of its object, as enlivens and invigorates its frame: and having overcome the opposition which this occasions, it sometimes imagines itself present in every part of the scene which it contemplates; and from the sense of this immensity, feels a noble pride, and entertains a lofty conception of its own capacity. (p. 12 [1. 2]).

Echoes of Baillie's phrasing are obvious. Gerard continues to follow Baillie by insisting on "simplicity." Only if the mind, undistracted by small parts, can "take in with ease one entire conception of [an] object," will "fancy . . . extend and enlarge . . . [this view] to infinity" (pp. 13–14 [1. 2]). Paradoxically, simplicity makes things easy for a mind that, nevertheless, spreads itself only with "difficulty" and gains a better opinion of itself for having done so. This is a difference from Baillie that Gerard may owe to Hume.[8] Gerard proceeds with the usual list of sublime objects: "the Alps, the Nile, the ocean, the wide expanse of heaven, . . . [and] the immensity of space uniformly extended without limit or termination" (p. 11 [1. 2]). Also, like Baillie, he finds sublimity in other "objects" with "the same power [as visible amplitude] to exalt the disposition of the observer." Various passions become sublime through the links of cause and effect, works of architecture through association with "strength and durableness," painting through its "expressiveness" of passion or quantity, literature through the association of words: "Seneca gives a sublime idea of Cicero's genius, by comparing it with the majesty and extent of the Roman Empire" (pp. 14–28 [1. 2]). Gerard's other illustrations are from Homer, Virgil, Horace,

Cicero, and Sannazar. None are from tragedy. But Gerard suggests some similarity to the tragic when he includes "loud roaring thunder" as arousing terror and therefore exciting sublime emotion. "For terror always implies astonishment, occupies the whole soul, and suspends all its motions" (p. 16 [1. 2]). To account for the resulting "awful sedateness," perhaps Gerard is thinking of some association with infinite power; but, as Monk points out (*Sublime*, p. 11), he does not say so. By classifying terror as sublime, Gerard is not following Baillie. A mind paralyzed by fear was not Baillie's idea of sublimity. Here Gerard is closer to Burke, but although Burke's *Enquiry* appeared two years before the *Essay on Taste*, there seems to be no other hint that Gerard had read it.

In general, except for a fuller account of literary effects, Gerard has followed Baillie rather closely in tracing emotional equivalence of size to association. But, whereas Baillie bases sublime feeling on sensory images extended by the imagination and describes association only as a means of bringing passions or small objects up to the emotional point where they offer an equivalent experience, Gerard allows association a greater contribution to sublimity. The association of cause and effect may not only establish qualitative or moral size but also add to the sublime pleasures of visual extension.[9] The effects of "power," "genius," and "vigours of mind" make these qualities as wonderful and astonishing as amplitude. But if this sort of excellence is combined with actual amplitude, the two kinds of sublimity reinforce each other.

> The greatness, for instance, of the works of nature, is considered as a striking indication of the omnipotence of their author. A vast fleet or army suggests an high opinion of the sovereign or the nation by whom they are provided or employed. In such cases, our admiration of the cause is excited by the view of the effect, and, being reflected back on the effect, heightens the sentiments of sublimity which it inspires. (P. 18 [1. 2])

In other words, the vast army (the effect) suggests a high opinion of the cause (some sort of excellence in the sovereign or nation), so that the cause excites greater admiration. At the same time, a high opinion of the cause (the excellence) makes the effect (the vast army) more admirable and therefore more sublimely pleasurable. From Addison's remark that vast objects give us a pleasing idea of God's infinite extent and power (*S.* 413), we might infer some sort of mutual reinforcing by cause and effect to enhance the pleasures of greatness. But Gerard is explicit on this score. The emotional interplay of cause and effect which he describes adds pleasure beyond that due to vastness or to its emotional equivalent; and in the dynamic modification of idea by idea, the immediate causes of sublime emotion attain an emotional "simplicity" not confined by topographical sameness. A dominant emotion will select and mold particulars, gaining power from the impact of each detail. This mental activity offers a psychological measure of sublimity that goes beyond the effects of visual extension.

Gerard has looked through a door that Alison would open thirty-one years later. But all we get from Gerard is a brief glimpse. Despite his tentative step toward freeing sublimity from the qualities of physical extension, Gerard stays close to Baillie in restricting the sublime to greatness in nature or its emotional equivalent.[10] As we shall see later, he must choose the "sense of imitation," rather than the sublime, to convert the tragic disagreeables.

3

Gerard's various pleasures of taste reinforce each other, but the pleasures of the sublime or of any other reflex sense or of all the reflex senses acting together are limited in their approach to truth by the limits Gerard sets for the imagination itself. These limits exclude the full operation of the moral faculty and reason. Into the ideas arousing sublime emotion, association more often than not must bring some kind of moral evaluation, but that is not to say that the whole moral faculty is involved. Gerard uses the term "moral sense" in two ways: (1) as a name for one of the seven internal senses making up the powers of the imagination, and (2) as a synonym for the "moral faculty," which directs or supervises the internal moral sense (pp. 189, 193 [3. 6]). Presumably the moral faculty, about which Gerard is not very specific, relies on reason to classify its experiences with pain and pleasure. At any rate, the moral faculty calls for mental resources not included in taste. By lending emotion to abstract moral sentiments, taste becomes an influence, although "not one of the most powerful," on morality; but "a careful examination of the moral faculty, would probably lead us to derive it from other principles than those from which taste has been explained" (pp. 186, 189, 194 [3. 6]). In his *Observations on Man* (1749), Hartley makes a similar distinction. The imagination whets the pleasures of morality by associating them with pleasing images, but it provides pleasures less intellectually demanding and therefore less enduring than those of the moral faculty.[11]

Taste can vivify but not match the powers and pleasures of either the moral faculty or reason. Judgment, or reason, is the faculty that compares, distinguishes, generalizes from empirical data, and engages in syllogistic proof (pp. 83; 176 [2. 2; 3. 4]).[12] Gerard assigns the rational faculty, along with the moral one, a higher rank than he gives the imagination or taste (p. 143 [4. 1]). In fact, he sometimes takes pains to dissociate imagination from reason. Like Addison, he finds the pleasures of taste "less improving than such as are intellectual. . . . The improvement of taste is easier, and more certain, than that of reason" (p. 182 [3. 5]). Judgment or "good sense," nevertheless, takes a hand in aesthetic matters. It discriminates, for the artist and critic alike, among the pleasures of taste and ranks some higher than others (p. 83 [2. 2]).[13] It adds to our enjoyment of each of the arts by discovering "the mutual connexion" among them. Within a specific work it looks at the relation of part to part, part to whole, means to ends, character to nature, character to character, character to action, character trait to character trait, sentiments to subject, style to custom (pp. 84–88 [2. 2]). This "conjunction of taste and reason" provides art with a pattern, varied yet uniform, which is pleasing in itself, but also "highly useful in science"; for, by making us feel "the *beauty*" of reason's deductions, it encourages "philosophical inquiries" and "heightens our convictions of [reasoned] conclusions" (p. 179 [3. 4]). Out of regard for orderly design, it provides intuitions of truth prior to rational examination. Gerard is suggesting the method of science whereby the investigator's conditioned imagination leads him to hypotheses which—even though they may be aesthetically pleasing— must then be accepted or rejected according to either deduction or experimental proof. Gerard has not built into the imagination a truth-finding power which imagination alone possesses, which only its language can accommodate, and which validates itself in the immediate effect of a work of art. Judgment remains a kind of monitor to keep the imagination from committing itself to "plausible fables" instead of "solid truths." Again, as in its partnership with the moral faculty, "taste exercises only a subordinate jurisdiction" (p. 178 [3. 4]).

4

Gerard, like Burke, finds pleasure in the agitating and presumably sublime terror of tragedy; but for the principal source of tragic pleasure he turns to the sense of imitation, for it is in *differing* from nature, he believes, that art gains its power to convert unpleasant emotions into pleasant ones. Imitation, we discover, supplies a number of the pleasures usually attributed to it: gratification "by a designed resemblance," satisfaction in the "gentle exercise" of comparison and in the "discovery of an original by a copy," and self-congratulation on "our own discernment and sagacity"—all supported by enjoyment of the artist's skill and ingenuity. The subject may be such that "other principles [of taste] concur to heighten its effect" of imitation; but "the force of imitation is most conspicuous" when it treats of "faulty originals" —the ugly, the irregular, the diseased, and the painful (pp. 47–48, 50–51 [1. 4]).

In his section "Of the Sense or Taste of Virtue" Gerard had already dealt with the ugly and the painful. The moral sense makes tragic materials pleasant through sympathy and a sense of justice consummated. With the success or defeat of virtue we enjoy, respectively, a "delightful serenity, complacence, and affiance in righteous providence" or "the pleasurable pain of compassion." With the triumph or punishment of vice, we "glow with indignation" or feel "the terrors of guilt" but "mix pity with our blame. We are thus agitated by those most important passions, the infusion of which constitutes the highest entertainment that works of taste can give" (pp. 70–71 [1. 7]). Without going into much detail, Gerard takes the best of both the affective and the fabulist worlds, but with his reliance on sympathy he clearly belongs in the former. Yet Gerard just as clearly found the affective hypothesis inadequate to account for the pleasures of tragedy. For a complete account, he had to turn to the sense that most obviously distinguishes art from actual life: that is, to the sense of imitation. Burke had attached little importance to imitation as a source of tragic pleasure. The power of tragedy "is more owing to the nature of the thing" imitated than to the pleasure of recognizing the reality in the imitation (*Enquiry*, pp. 49–50 [1. 16]). For Gerard, however, an imitation of a tragic action is enjoyable because it changes the nature of the thing imitated to conform to laws peculiar to a work of art.

In the Appendix added to the third edition of the *Essay* (1780) Gerard distinguishes between the kinds of imitation in dramatic and in nondramatic poetry. In the former, the imitation is "an exact copy" of persons acting and speaking. In the latter, the imitation is an "idea" or "general representation" in the mind of the poet. This idea is rendered exciting by the poet's delineation of certain objects, but the poem is not an imitation of these objects in the sense that a painting is an imitation of a landscape or a play an imitation of "conversation and actions" (pp. 276–83). There is at least room to doubt that Gerard had this distinction firmly in mind when he wrote the chapter on imitation first published in 1759. In any case, the kind of imitation he describes in the following passage would seem to be the pictorial or dramatic sort. It nevertheless involves—as in any work of art—the idealization inherent in Gerard's definition of taste, that is, the representation of objects as they appear to internal senses and, therefore, the emotional modification of one idea by another.

> The rudest rocks and mountains; the objects that in nature are most deformed; even disease and pain, acquire beauty when skilfully imitated in painting. . . . A perfect imitation of characters morally evil, can make us dwell with pleasure on them, notwithstanding the uneasy sentiments of disapprobation and abhorrence which they excite. The character of Iago is detestable, but we admire Shakespear's representation of it. Nay, imperfect and mixt characters are, in all kinds of writing, preferred to faultless ones, as being juster copies of real nature. The pleasant sensation resulting from the imitation is so intense, that it overpowers and converts into delight even the *uneasy* impressions which spring from the objects imitated. There can be no stronger proof of the force of imitation in conferring on its effects the power of pleasing, than its rendering those passions agreeable, when excited by it, which, when produced in the natural way, are pure and unmixed pain. Suspense, anxiety, terror, when produced in tragedy, by imitation of their objects and causes, and infused by sympathy, afford not only a more serious, but a much intenser and nobler satisfaction, than all the laughter and joy which farce or comedy can inspire. When thus secondarily produced, they agitate and employ the mind, and rouse and give scope to its greatest activity; while, at the same time, our implicit knowledge that the occasion is remote or fictitious, enables the pleasure of imitation to relieve the pure torment which would attend their primary operation (pp. 51–52 [1. 4]).[14]

Here are some old acquaintances: the recognition of an accurate copy, intense excitement and the resulting mental activity, and the comfort of remoteness or fictitiousness. The "conversion" of unpleasant emotions, however, is more interesting. Evil characters, despite the abhorrence they excite, add to our enjoyment because our recognition of their reality overcomes their noxiousness. In fact, our abhorrence—now converted by the pleasure of imitation—adds its intensity to that pleasure. The unpleasantness of terror is likewise converted by (1) our recognition that the characters are "just copies of nature" caught up by and appropriately responding to a probable sequence of events; (2) sympathy with these characters resulting in various moral feelings; and, presumably, (3) some of the sublime astonishment that, according to Gerard in an earlier chapter, always accompanies terror. Although in this particular passage Gerard does not explicitly say so, the sense of beauty must certainly help in the conversion by relating parts to the whole and means to ends (p. 49 [1. 4]), while probably harmony, novelty, and perhaps even ridicule have their share in pleasantly activating the mind.

Gerard's process of conversion recalls Hume's essay "Of Tragedy," published two years before the *Essay on Taste*. Just as the orator's "eloquence" renders melancholy materials pleasing to the audience, says Hume, so does tragedy— through "the force of imagination, the energy of expression, the power of numbers, the charms of imitation," set up a "prevailing movement" of emotion that, rather than diminishing the painful feelings, "converts" them to pleasant ones and adds their force to the overall effect of pleasure.[15] It is not necessary, therefore, for the critic to treat unpleasant materials as though they were encountered in actual life and thus, in order to find them pleasing, to put them at a distance in time, space, or reality. If evil is put at a distance, it is only that "distance" which always distinguishes art from actuality. The emotional force need not be weakened but only brought into line with the "sentiments of beauty" that dominate a work of art. The pleasure of tragedy is not limited to sympathy with afflicted characters, or to a feeling of security from pain, or to satisfaction with poetic justice, but, rather, it exists primarily in the mind's total response, with its harmonized emotions, to the work of art.[16] In other words, conversion adds to the pleasures of imitation the pleasure of creating something different from the thing imitated.

Although both Hume and Gerard attribute conversion to the imagination,[17] Gerard is more specific in explaining the imagination's dependence on association to modify ideas within the imaginative complex.[18] A pleasant emotion initially excited in a "complex perception" may resist the force of related ideas to change it, so that we ascribe pleasant feelings to the related ideas even though, in isolation, they would produce unpleasant ones. Conversely, the introductory perception may be made stronger, more agreeable, or even disagreeable by the ideas it introduces (pp. 157–60 [3. 1]). This process, obviously, must turn the sublime into the pathetic. A perception, strongly agreeable or disagreeable, will communicate its qualities to an associated perception less strong. Therefore "the strength and vivacity" of our perception (as of a tragic character, presumably) will arouse sympathy strong enough to enliven "our *ideas* of the passions infused by it to such a pitch, as in a manner converts them into the passions themselves" (p. 160). Gerard would not have subscribed to the distinction, made half a century later by Payne Knight, between sharing terror and pity and sympathizing only with the tragic character's "expression of passion, and mental energy."[19] Gerard could not allow the audience's sympathy to restrict itself to the character's energetic qualities. Sympathy must lead to sharing the character's feeling of fear, but at the same time it renders the feeling of fear enjoyable.

"Perhaps," F. L. Lucas has said, "Hume tends to think a little too much of the part played in Tragedy by eloquence . . . to see quite steadily the Muse herself."[20] Gerard, with his greater emphasis on the convincing representation of character, is more in the direction that the later criticism of tragedy was to take. Hume's theory of tragedy was criticized, in his own time, as precluding an intuitive response,[21] but neither Hume nor Gerard assumed any intermediate act of comparing or reflecting prior to feeling the force of a tragedy. As evident in Hume but more clearly stated by Gerard, the distressing passions are not isolated but immediately modified and rendered pleasant in the flow of associated ideas. It is not necessary, therefore, for Gerard to narrow the range of tragic materials to ensure a pleasant effect—that is, like Campbell, White, Blair, and Aikin, to argue for restraining the element of horror.[22] The limitation of horror, Aikin realized, poses a problem, for the restraint also may reduce the impulses of morality.[23] Gerard avoids this dilemma. His emphasis in his chapters on both beauty and imitation is clearly on evaluating the parts in relation to their total effect and not on measuring the parts by extrinsic standards of sensibility or decorum. He has no use for such "false delicacy" as Rymer's disgust "with the cunning and villany of Iago, as unnatural and absurd, soldiers being commonly described with openness and honesty of character" (p. 120 [2. 5]). He is occupied not with enfeebling the shocking materials but with showing how their force increases the enjoyment of the whole tragedy.

Gerard offers a useful, if limited, approach to tragedy. Like Burke he makes it unnecessary for the action to display Providence at work. Not that Gerard himself went so far as to remove the moral emotions of tragedy from providential concern, but his theory of conversion would accommodate this divorce and the tragedies in which it has taken place. He resembles Burke in putting a premium on emotional force and unity, but he is also respectful of well-ordered action. In recognizing that the pleasures of tragedy differ in kind from those offered by violence or destruction in actual life, he departs from Burke. In founding the sublime on fear, says A. C. Bradley, Burke recognizes only the first of the two stages which Kant finds in encountering the sublime. These are, in Bradley's own terms, (1) "a sense [if only for a fraction of a second] of being checked, or baffled, or even stupefied, or possibly even repelled or menaced, as though something were affecting us which we could not receive, or grasp, or stand up to," and (2) "a powerful reaction, a rush of self-expression, or an uplifting, a sense of being borne out of the self that was checked, or even of being carried beyond all checks and limits."[24] In itself, actual fear, according to Bradley, is never sublime. If we are to achieve the second stage, fear "must be changed in character." Burke, of course, had already changed the character of fear by removing the immediate threat of danger so that the "astonishment" which fills the mind is delightful. Gerard, on the other hand, does not handle tragic fear as though it arose from a threat to one's actual safety. He changes the character of fear in a manner peculiar to art, thus opening the mind to "a rush of self-expression." The motions of the mind, far from being arrested, are extended in the flow of associated ideas, modifying each other through strong emotion.

Gerard, however, put a ceiling on the mind's expansion. Just because of their peculiarity to a work of art, the expansive pleasures of tragedy suffer certain limitations. The pleasures of taste may be "as great" as intellectual pleasures but are "less improving"; they make morality attractive but offer no moral insights. So when Gerard says that the pleasures of tragedy "give scope to the mind's greatest activity," he is not including the full powers of reason and the moral faculty. The "mind's activity" looks as if it were "greatest" in dealing with indolence and languor rather than with ignorance. Even though it rises partly from moral sympathy under the surveillance of judgment, all this activity seems inadequate to lift any considerable weight of pain. Although he assigns the highest truths to deductive reason, Gerard, in his definition of taste, has thrown away the lever of deduction. Yet with his trains of wide-ranging ideas mutually modified into an immediate simplicity, Gerard has set up an admirable psychological operation potentially useful for the rational yet immediate confrontation of evil—and thus for attaining the knowledge that is not possible apart from tragedy.

CHAPTER FIVE

ALISON

Archibald Alison has been credited with subjectivizing the sublime.[1] As we have seen, Dennis, Addison, Baillie, Burke, and Gerard all make complex ideas the immediate cause of sublime emotions; but all except Dennis trace these emotions to the idea itself rather than to the process of forming it. Whatever association adds to the idea is often considered necessary to bring it up, emotionally, to the sublime size of visible objects. The visible remains the ultimate test of sublimity. By giving a broader sanction to association, Alison opens the way to the *sublime of vision*, which demands a much greater contribution from the mind than the visible sublime requires. Alison ascribes aesthetic pleasure entirely to the process of association. Thus the immediately visible, while necessary to initiate this process, becomes subordinate to the range of mental activity that it stimulates.

Ascribed to the process of association rather than to visible objects, the sublime loses some pecularities that had tended to keep it distinct from the tragic. Since association extends thought as well as emotion, the sublime acquires rational insight. As association, under the direction of power-

69

ful feeling, brings a variety of experiences into order, the mind can organize even the destructive forces in human life. We discover, when we come to Alison's brief excursion into practical criticism, that his own organization of the evil he finds in tragedy is not very firm; but his theory, which others would put to better use, is not at fault. A second peculiarity of the sublime that Alison gets rid of is the religious burden inherited from the natural sublime. Alison does not deny that the sublime is religious, but he believes that all aesthetic experience is religious because it testifies to God's beneficence in endowing the human mind with creative power. Alison's emphasis, here as always, is on what the *mind* contributes. Religious force is not inherent in genre but in the artist. In the third place, Alison frees the sublime in art from restrictions originally found in visible mass. The sort of unity that sublime art attains comes from the mind; it is not patterned after externals. This unity is not "uniformity or regularity" in time or space but "unity of emotion," which characterizes the best in both dramatic and nondramatic poetry.

1

Like Gerard, Alison was a Scottish minister who is remembered for a book on taste. He published his *Essays on the Nature and Principles of Taste* in Edinburgh in 1790. Although favorably reviewed, the book did not require a second edition until 1811. Four more Edinburgh editions appeared by 1825. These *Essays*—which are perhaps best known through Jeffrey's 1811 review and for their influence on Wordsworth—had considerable effect on contemporary thought.[2] Alison is the most consistent of eighteenth-century writers on the sublime in translating the sublime, and the beautiful as well, into psychological terms—that is, in seeing all aesthetic experience as comprising trains of associated ideas and the accompanying emotions. For Alison, sublimity and beauty do not inhere in any external object but depend entirely on association. "The qualities of matter are in themselves incapable of producing emotion . . . yet . . . from their association with other qualities" they become "signs or expressions" of emotion-exciting qualities (pp. 106–107 [essay 2, chap. 1]).[3] The term *association,* as Alison uses it, seems to include all the relationships of resemblance, contiguity, and cause and effect stated by Hume;[4] but "the principal relationship" in these aesthetic trains is "resemblance; the relation . . . the most loose and general, and . . . [affording] the greatest range of thought for our imagination to pursue" (p. 23 [essay 1, chap. 1, sec. 2]). The "emotion of taste"— which is Alison's term for aesthetic experience—goes beyond "the simple perception of the object" to embrace a whole complex of associated images, thoughts, and emotions assembled by the imagination.

> Thus, when we feel either the beauty or sublimity of natural scenery—the gay lustre of a morning in spring, or the mild radiance of a summer evening, the savage majesty of a wintry storm, or the wild magnificence of a tempestuous ocean—we are conscious of a variety of images in our minds, very different from those which the objects themselves can present to the eye. Trains of pleasing or of solemn thought arise spontaneously within our minds; our hearts swell with emotions, of which the objects before us seem to afford no adequate cause. . . . (P. 18 [1. 1. 1])

These trains may probe into the mind's intellectual and moral resources. In a passage recalling Hobbes's distinction between "unguided" and "regulated" trains of thought and Lord Kames's "reverie,"[5] and anticipating Hazlitt's "disinterestedness" and Keats's "negative capability," Alison writes: "That state of mind . . . is most favourable to the emotions of taste, in which the imagination is free and unembarrassed" by any practical or rational purpose (pp. 20–21 [1. 1. 2]). However, it would be inaccurate to conclude that "Alison makes taste entirely dependent on the imagination, to the exclusion of judgment and reason."[6] Of course taste does not include the construction of syllogisms. The cognition that Alison includes as part of the aesthetic experience is a process which, although comprising both the specific and the general, continually fuses the two. It cannot be recorded in a series of propositions but only in association-laden particulars. For Alison, as for such others before him as Sir Joshua Reynolds and Abraham Tucker, the imagination, without any effort of the will, draws on accumulated experience for comparisons and generalizations, to become thereby an act of immediate cognition as well as pleasure.[7] Alison's trains include "pleasing or solemn thoughts" and "analogies with the life of man." Autumn scenes, for instance, inspire "that current of thought, which, from such appearances of decay, so naturally leads him to the solemn imagination of that inevitable fate, which is to bring on alike the decay of life, of empire, and of nature itself" (p. 24 [1. 1. 2]). Rendered intuitive by experience, these comparisons and generalizations come "immediately." The same kinds of trains characterize our enjoyment of painting, music, or poetry (p. 18 [1. 1. 1]). Alison's insistence on the subjectivity of beauty and sublimity casts some doubt on the objective truth of these comparisons and generalizations, but nevertheless Alison assumes, as a stable base for the highest aesthetic pleasure, a network of associations that is widely shared, at least among the educated and leisured classes (pp. 60–61 [1. 2. 2]; pp. 303–304 [2. 4. 3]).

Alison also finds a strong moral and religious component in the "emotion of taste." That beauty and sublimity depend on an "expression of the mind" rather than any quality inhering in an object is, in fact, evidence of God's beneficence as the final cause of aesthetic pleasure. Even "the rocks and the deserts" nurturing a savage will have pleasing associations for him; and the marks of age or disease, rather than disfiguring a loved one, will become signs of the lasting affection that cements pleasure to the principles of duty. The "Divine artist" has endowed us with susceptibility to moral feelings, which association then comes to bind with certain objects, animate or inanimate. "While the objects of the material world are made to attract our infant eyes, there are latent ties by which they reach our hearts; and wherever they afford us delight, they are always the signs or expressions of higher qualities, by which our moral sensibilities are called forth (pp. 423–24, 428 [2. 6. 6]). The "latent ties" imply, it would seem, not some power inherent in the object—which Alison always denies—but a disposition in the child, antedating any association, to respond to certain objects with a kind of pleasure that purifies the mind of evil. Once the object and the moral pleasure have been associated, this and similar objects continue to provide moral strength. Like the "high objects" Wordsworth mentions in *The Prelude* as "purifying . . . / The elements of feeling and of thought," they may be recalled in "maturer seasons" (bk. 1, ll. 410–11, 595) to reinforce, according to Alison, "those sentiments and principles" which bring happiness to others and honor to ourselves. This "great purpose of nature" is "yet more evident" in the sublimity and beauty of works of art and most evident in the sympathetic virtues expressed by *"the human countenance and form."* Ultimately, as signs of God's power, wisdom, and goodness, beauty and sublimity lead us "directly to RELIGIOUS sentiment" (pp. 429–30 [2. 6. 6]).

2

Aesthetic pleasure is increased by "additional trains of imagery" (pp. 37, 48 [1. 1. 3]), which in turn depend upon "the degree in which . . . uniformity of character prevails" (p. 24 [1. 1. 2]). Or, to use a term that Alison shares with earlier writers on the sublime, this expansion of the mind depends on *simplicity*. In itself, Alison's distinction between the effects of beauty and of sublimity is commonplace enough. Like others, Alison traces aesthetic experience to sounds and, more especially, to "objects of sight." "Fine and winding lines" are most beautiful since they are associated with delicacy and ease, while "strong and angular lines" are least beautiful, since they express "harshness, roughness, etc." (pp. 186–87, 206 [2. 4. 1]). Beautiful sounds, too, are rather gentle, familiar, and undisturbing: "the sound of a waterfall, the murmuring of a rivulet, the whispering of the wind, the sheepfold bell, the sound of the curfew, &c." (p. 124 [2. 2. 1]). On the other hand, as one might expect, the pleasures of sublimity are more intense. Sublime sounds are associated with "ideas of danger, or power, or majesty, &c." Thunder, for its expression of awe and terror, is the most sublime of the sounds in nature (pp. 114–15 [2. 2. 1]). Sublime forms, which also express "qualities capable of exciting very strong emotions," include bodies having "magnitude" of height, depth, breadth, or length, or "bodies connected . . . with ideas of Danger or Power" (military weapons), with "great duration" (Gothic castles), with "splendour or magnificence" (thrones, triumphal arches), and with "awe or solemnity" (temples, religious services, Jupiter's thunderbolts, the Heavens) (pp. 178–82 [2. 4. 1]). In its references to size and power, especially with religious significance, Alison's list of sublime objects and qualities is hardly unique. What is not commonplace is Alison's explanation of sublime mind-stretching in exclusively psychological terms, that is, his substitution of psychological size for physical size. Although he may still describe sublime forms in terms drawn from the usual kinds of magnitude, he does not burden the sublime in art with restrictions based on measurements in time and space. He can therefore attribute sublimity to a mass of images with its own kind of unity or "simplicity."

"Simplicity" as freedom from small or distracting detail had often been considered important to the sublime. The disposition to link the sublime with the general rather than the particular has been traced by Scott Elledge, who points out that Longinus himself found an enumeration of "things productive of smallness in detail" antithetical to the "noble and sublime."[8] The natural sublime made simplicity something visual, as evident in Addison and especially in Baillie and Gerard. Addison cites the "poor and weak Effects" of the excessive detail in a "Gothick Cathedral" compared with the "Greatness of the Manner" that distinguishes the *Pantheon at Rome*" (*Spectator* 415). According to Baillie and Gerard, small or dissimilar parts trip up the imagination as it attempts to rush out into space.[9] Samuel Johnson's well-known comment on "the grandeur of generality" in the *Life of Cowley* expresses the usual concern for sublime "aggregation" unbroken by "minuteness" and for a "comprehension and expanse of thought which at once fills the whole mind." Johnson seems to refer both to visual extension ("the prospects of nature" and "the wide effulgence of a summer noon") and to widely general thoughts ("not limited by exceptions"). The integrity of the former must not be broken by distracting detail, and its inclusiveness must not be limited by nonrepresentative particulars.[10]

Alison, too, makes simplicity necessary to the kind of mind-stretching he requires of both sublimity and beauty, that is, to an extended concatenation of associated images—an extension that enriches the aesthetic experience with habitual thought and feeling. For Alison, simplicity is unity of emotion or unity of "character." It is one of the two qualities that distinguish aesthetic trains from "ordinary" ones, the other quality being the "simple emotion" excited by each idea within the train (pp. 51–55 [1. 2. 2]).

> In those trains . . . suggested by objects of sublimity or beauty . . . there is always some general principle of connexion which pervades the whole, and gives them some certain and definite character. They are either gay, or pathetic, or melancholy, or solemn, or awful, or elevating, &c. according to the nature of the emotion which is first excited. Thus the prospect of a serene evening in summer, produces first an emotion of peacefulness and tranquillity, and then suggests a variety of images corresponding to this primary impression. (P. 55 [1. 2. 1])

The delight attending "every operation of taste" is not merely the sum of the simple emotions produced by each image or idea but includes "a higher and more pleasing kind" attributable to the exercise of the imagination as it produces a unified train (pp. 98–99 [1. Conclusion]). This kind of pleasure increases as the imagination extends itself to supply "additional trains of imagery" (p. 48 [1. 1. 3]) directed, of course by the emotion "first excited." "When our hearts are affected, we seek only for objects congenial to our emotion: and the simplicity . . . [of a landscape or painting permits] us to indulge, without interruption, those interesting trains of thought which the character of the scene is fitted to inspire" (p. 82 [1. 2. 3]). This simplicity, with the additional trains it permits, is required of both beauty and sublimity; but since sublime emotions are more intense than those excited by beauty and since aesthetic emotions are proportioned to "uniformity of character" and to the "range of thought" it encourages (p. 23 [1. 1. 2]), one might infer that sublimity calls on the imagination to produce the more abundant trains.

Alison distinguishes "simplicity" from "uniformity or regularity," such as that of primitive art. He prefers the greater detail, variety, and realism of modern art, as long as the details are selected in "accord with the general expression of the scene" (pp. 78; 258–60 [1. 2. 3; 2. 4. 2]). This same sort of simplicity is as necessary in poetry as in painting. In fact, it is more important to the poet, who must blend together qualities perceived not only by sight but by other senses and, in addition, "the sublimity and beauty of the moral and intellectual world" (p. 83 [1. 2. 3]). Alison applies this requirement not only to descriptive poetry but "to every other branch of poetical imitation, to the description of characters, the sentiments, and the passions of men." "The same unity of emotion is demanded in dramatic poetry, at least in the highest and noblest species of it, tragedy" (pp. 91–92, 94 [1. 2. 3]). Of course, Kames and other associationist critics had suggested kinds of unity based on relations other than the more formal ones of time, place, and action; and Kames had also found "simplicity . . . a chief property" of tragedy if its subject is to occupy "our whole attention." But in this context "simplicity" apparently depends on unity of action, which for Kames remains the most important kind in tragedy.[11] However, for Alison, "unity of character," along with the emotional abundance it promotes, is "fully as essential as any of those three unities, of which every book of criticism is so full" (p. 94 [1. 2. 3]). Indeed, Alison's emphasis usually makes it seem a good deal more essential.

3

But Alison's sublime pleasures of tragedy, like Burke's,

are still mainly, if not entirely, emotional. Although he defines the imagination as offering, in the immediate impact of a work of art, knowledge derived through comparison and generalization, Alison makes little use of this cognitive power in defining the pleasures of tragedy. The moral force of tragedy is derived not from better understanding of pain and death but—as in Burke—from the kind of emotions tragedy evokes. To this extent, at least, Alison identifies the sublime with the pathetic. At its best, tragedy awakens "only the greatest and noblest passions of the human soul," thus rendering the theater "a school of sublime instruction" (p. 95 [1. 2. 3]).

Hence the need for unity of emotion or character. Alison's elevation of this kind of unity does not, however, lead him to make very liberal judgments. He finds tragicomedy, for want of unified character, "utterly indefensible" and, therefore, Shakespeare's taste inferior to his genius. For "an uniform character of dignity," Alison therefore turns to a writer with more classical tastes and a concern for *all* the unities: that is, to Corneille, who disregarded "whatever of common, of trivial, or even of pathetic in the originals from which he copied" that might distract us from the "greatest and noblest passions." Without citing any of Corneille's works, Alison admits his "extravagance and bombast" but would make "some allowance . . . for a poet, who first shewed to his country the example of regular tragedy" (pp. 95–96 [1. 2. 3]).

Alison's lack of confidence in the fusing power of the imagination, despite his able argument for this power, appears again when he explains how the evil characters in tragedy contribute to tragic pleasure. In his Introduction, Alison proposes to examine "the qualities of sublimity and beauty . . . in objects that are in themselves productive of PAIN" (p. viii). As it turns out, he never does this in any systematic way, but he provides some scattered comments that help in guessing how he would have analyzed this kind of enjoyment. The usual delight in perceiving an accurate imitation—which Alison dismisses as a "cold pleasure"—would have played but a small part. Instead, the emotional contribution to expressing "one pure and unmingled character" would have been the important thing. To be pleasing in a work of art, an object, viewed in the context of that work, only has to have associations that contribute to the delightful emotion characterizing the whole scene, picture, or person. As one learns to appreciate art for "character" rather than for mere imitation, he comes to enjoy even "the representation of desert or of desolate prospects" for its characterizing feeling of solitude, desolation, or wildness (pp. 81–82 [1. 2. 3]). Similarly, the withered signs of age, or the honorable scars of combat, may characterize the portrait of a beloved friend or a national hero (pp. 372, 388–90, 395 [2. 6. 3–4]). This contribution of unpleasant materials to an overall effect of pleasure is not quite the same as the "conversion" of feeling described by Hume and Gerard, according to whom painful feelings in tragedy are pleasantly resolved by the "prevailing" emotions of imitation, energy of expression, power of numbers, etc. Thus, the emotions of terror and moral disapproval are changed qualitatively and add their component, quantitatively, to the general pleasure.[12] For Alison, however, the somber materials contribute an emotional force which has been determined qualitatively by previous experience and which adds directly, or by contrast, to the prevailing effect.

When it comes to immoral beings rather than harsh scenery or mere physical decay, Alison uses the principle of contrast to justify the expression of "dark, or malignant, or selfish affections." The beauty of the "representation of *Richard* or *Iago*" lies in the contrast that "gives effect to the character and the expression of virtue." That is, the representation of such characters has only the "artificial" beauty appropriate to the purpose of the composition. Attitudes and gestures which are "beautiful in themselves" are those that express "amiable dispositions," i.e., those of "gaiety, gentleness, pity, humility, &c.," and not those expressing "fear, rage, envy, pride, cruelty, &c." (pp. 389–90 [2. 6. 4]). Richard III and Iago are, of course, about as villainous as tragic characters are likely to become. Alison does not discuss the kind of character whose attitudes and gestures express both good and bad qualities. In such a character, perhaps, he would see the evil as making the good stand out more clearly.

As this shift in standards of beauty from harsh objects in external nature to harsh passions in human nature suggests, the unifying emotion does not have quite the same components in dramatic as in descriptive poetry. As we have seen, God—by providing "latent ties" between "our hearts" and the "objects of the material world" and, in addition, the capacity to store up associations—has made these material objects a continual source of moral delight and religious sentiment. Even the harsher natural objects have their place in supplying aesthetic pleasure for the local inhabitants and for the more sophisticated tastes that have learned to enjoy unified scenes of desolation, danger, and wildness. God has also accommodated our aesthetic emotions to the physical signs of disease or age; but unlike "the rocks and deserts" and "the collapsed cheek," the "attitudes and gestures" expressing fear, rage, and cruelty are not susceptible to pleasant associations. According to Alison's aesthetic, a play comprising only, or mainly, evil characters doing evil acts could not be enjoyable, for despite the unified expression of character, the "simple ideas" comprised by the trains would be unpleasant. For Alison, unpleasant ideas find a place in tragedy only because, by contrast, they intensify the pleasure derived from the amiable ideas and the trains comprising them. Alison takes no notice of the possibility that the unpleasant ideas, in the context of imaginative trains, might become enjoyable through a recognition of their truth, an awareness of their place in human life, or their reconciliation with Providence. The idea of Providence yielded by taste is, like that supplied by Addison's "greatness," without benefit of reason: God's benignity is clear in nature's offering of moral pleasures. But Alison's further suggestion that evil in tragedy makes good more attractive is hardly one that he could have used to explain evil in actual life. He would have had to make that explanation in terms not admitted to his definition of taste. Perhaps Alison would have dealt more satisfactorily with the problem of evil if he had completed that part of the *Essays* which was to deal with those "noblest productions of the fine arts . . . founded upon subjects of TERROR and DIS- TRESS" (p. viii, Introduction). As the *Essays* stand, Alison tells us little about the sharing or the conversion of these agitating emotions.

4

In Alison we find another step—beyond Burke and Ge- rard—in identifying the sublime and the tragic. Alison is not unusual, of course, in finding sublimity an intense sort of aesthetic experience, tragedy an intense sort of poetry, and therefore a close relationship between the sublime and the tragic. He is unusual, rather, for breaking the sublime free from limitations imposed by its early union with large ob- jects. He succeeded in divorcing "uniformity" or "simplicity" from visual patterns easily repeated by the imagination. In their insistence on a visual uniformity, Addison, Baillie, and Gerard had overlooked or underestimated the power of asso- ciated images to modify each other emotionally and to pro- duce, thereby, an emotional simplicity not dependent on scenic regularity. Thus emotion organizes a kind of vastness quite different from that of external objects: a psychological magnitude comprising a wide range of images with their ac- companying thoughts and feelings. Far from being impaired by abundant and varied particulars, this sort of magnitude thrives on them. Not blunted by vagueness, these particulars thrust their associations into a binding interplay of sensation, thought, and emotion. Varied or sharp details, therefore, do not hinder aggregation; nor, since Alison assumes a network of associations shared by an educated and leisured audience, do they check the response short of generality. This sort of psychological mass delights the mind more fully, and in dif- ferent ways, from a complex idea of visual size.

A sublime not dominated by ideas of physical size would more readily merge with the tragic. In size and integrity of psychological mass, Alison sees no difference between descriptive and dramatic poetry. Nor does he see why, when it comes to religious sentiment, one genre should have an inherent advantage over another. Furthermore, in theory at least, he would allow the imagination to amass "solemn thoughts" of a depth appropriate to tragedy. Nevertheless, Alison is a little disappointing when it comes to the thought that he himself finds in tragedy. He has no difficulty explaining the pleasure derived from the harsher aspects of material objects: all of these may be beautiful or—more likely—sublime in their contribution to the moral pleasure of an emotionally integrated scene, painting, or description. Alison has satisfactorily integrated such aspects with his own conception of God's benevolent design; for, he points out, divine benevolence has made all kinds of material objects susceptible to pleasing associations. But this cannot be true of evil actions. Therefore, the evil characters in tragedy have only an "artificial" kind of beauty derived from their power to increase, by contrast, the amiable pleasures of viewing the good characters. In his analysis of the pleasures of tragedy, Alison does not come to grips with the problem of evil in human life or with the function of tragedy in defining the role of evil.

Nevertheless, Alison helps lay the psychological basis for a more penetrating treatment of evil in Hazlitt and Keats. Aesthetic pleasure, he says, increases as the imagination's trains—speeding along the same emotional track—range most widely, and bring into the complex of ideas more and more of our accumulated experience and the resulting thoughts and feeling, finding more analogies between visual images and "the life of man," exercising "our moral sensibility," and "leading us directly to RELIGIOUS sentiment." Although the hampering restraints of reason and judgment are lifted during the reverie necessary to extended trains, previous conclusions of reason and judgment are nevertheless available for fusion within the imaginative complex. It might be concluded, therefore, that even the grimmest aspects of human as well as material nature—seen, known, and evaluated in and through this complex—could become pleasing. But, ignoring the cognitive power he has found in the imaginative process and perhaps content with amiable religious sentiment strengthened by contrast with evil, Alison does not reach this conclusion.

CHAPTER SIX

KNIGHT

In identifying the tragic with the sublime, Richard Payne Knight seems in some ways more modern than Alison. Firmly separating art from actual life and insisting on the amorality of art, Knight finds malignant characters aesthetically acceptable because the audience enjoys sharing the energy of their passions and not because, as Alison believes, they make the virtue displayed in a tragedy seem more beautiful by contrast. This emphasis on a feeling of power derived from sharing energetic passions seems to bring Knight closer in phrasing and thought, as well as in time, to Hazlitt. But in a more important sense—insofar as the narrative traced in this study is concerned—Knight represents a turn backward toward Burke and older definitions of sublimity. Knight takes issue with Burke on many points, but he extends the affective hypothesis into the nineteenth century. He sees the tragic disagreeables overcome by sympathetic emotion and by sympathetic emotion alone. Knight goes beyond Burke in the importance that he assigns to association, but the enrichment of aesthetic experience by trains of ideas does not enrich sublimity with knowledge of good and evil. Although sublime ideas must be constructed by association, ultimately they offer the same limited sort of pleasure as visible size.

1

The Landscape, a Didactic Poem in Three Books, Addressed to Uvedale Price, Esq. (1794) engaged Knight in a controversy with Price and with Humphry Repton regarding the picturesque. Knight's *Analytical Inquiry into the Principles of Taste* (1805) also deals with the picturesque, but its importance to the present study lies mainly in the final part, which finds sublimity in good tragedy. The *Analytical Inquiry* comprises three parts: on sensation, the association of ideas, and the passions.[1] In Part 3 Knight makes it clear that he is concerned with the passions only insofar as they are part of aesthetic experience. "The passions, considered either physically as belonging to the constitution of the individual, or morally, as operating upon that of society, do not come within the scope of my present inquiry; it being only by sympathy, that they are connected with subjects of taste; or that they produce, in the mind, any of those tender feelings, which are called pathetic, or those exalted or enthusiastic sentiments, which are called sublime" (p. 315 [pt. 3, chap. 1, sec. 1]). Like Johnson, Knight makes both "the pathetic" and "the sublime" *pathetic* in the sense that they represent feelings shared by a sympathetic audience. But he does not separate these feelings, as Johnson does, according to whether they are stimulated by human life or by nature.[2] In fact he hardly separates them at all except by their respective origins in the extremes of tenderness or destructiveness. It is only in actual life—and not always there—that the pathetic and the sublime may be kept apart. "In all the fictions, either of poetry or imitative art, there can be nothing truly pathetic unless it be, at the same time, in some degree, sublime." The pathetic, although nonviolent, is not to be confused with any sort of weakness. Without "a display of vigour," tenderness and sensibility in fiction will invite only scorn (p. 354–55 [3.

1. 41]). Tragedy, therefore, invites the audience to share both tender vigor and violent energy.

Although in tragedy the pathetic and the sublime make themselves felt through sympathy, the feeling that the audience shares with the characters is not—as it would be if the characters were real—with their "actual distress" (p. 327 [3. 1. 14]). "Subjects of taste" differ from reality. The "truth or falsehood" of a work of art is tested, not by closeness to practical experience, but by the consistency of its parts; and its pleasures, far from being those of actual life on a diminished scale, are of a different kind altogether. Knight, unlike Burke, does not see tragedy becoming more powerful as it approaches actuality. If, as Burke says, an audience would get up and leave " 'the most sublime and affecting tragedy' " to watch the execution of " 'a state criminal of high rank . . . in an adjoining square,' " it is a "triumph as much of curiosity, as of sympathy," since the execution of such a criminal has become a rare event (pp. 316–17 [3. 1. 1–4]).[3] The aim of tragedy is not to duplicate the emotional effects of an execution but to awaken "exquisite and delightful thrills of sympathy" by "the motives, for which . . . [distress] is endured; the exertions, which it calls forth; and the sentiments of heroism, fortitude, constancy, or tenderness, which it, in consequence, displays" (pp. 327–28 [3. 1. 14]). In a substantial portion of Part 3, Chapter 1, Knight attacks Burke's proposition that a shared emotion of terror excited by *"ideas of pain and danger"* is a source of the sublime: even *"at certain distances"* or in *"certain degrees"* pain and danger cannot be delightful, for "danger means the probability of evil, and pain the actual sensation of it" (pp. 372–73 [3. 1. 60–61]).[4] Knight would agree with Baillie that the agitation of terror is unpleasant enough to destroy a feeling of sublimity.[5] But, Knight says, the audience is saved from such unpleasant sympathy by its knowledge that what it is watching is merely a fiction. Otherwise, "the sufferings, which we beheld, would excite such a painful degree of sympathy, as would overpower and suppress the pleasant feelings, excited by the noble, tender, or generous sentiments, which we heard uttered" (p. 329 [3. 1. 15]).

Knight, then, takes issue with Aristotle—and with Dryden and Dennis—on the excitation of terror and pity and on the moral effects of these emotions. "How any man, in his senses, can feel either fear from dangers, which he knows to be unreal; or commiseration for distress, which he knows to be fictitious, I am at a loss to discover." What the audience sympathizes with, rather, are "the expressions of passion, and mental energy, which those fictitious events excite" (p. 330 [3. 1. 16]). To support his position, Knight cites Longinus, who found *"the passions of grief, sorrow, fear, &c. . . . incapable . . . of producing any sublime effect"* (p. 331 [3. 1. 17]).[6] These passions, whether arising out of one's own suffering or sympathy with others' distress, are basically selfish, and along with all sorts of "whining complaints" or "sordid sensuality" are not sufficiently elevated to qualify as either pathetic or sublime. Pathetic and sublime emotions are excited only by "just and appropriate expression of energetic passion." This expression may be found not only in "sentiments of rapturous and enthusiastic affection . . . highly elevated above every thing selfishly low or sordid," but also in the opposite of love: "hatred or malignity." The only absolute necessity is that the passions expressed be "decisive and energetic." No "degree of coldness, weakness, or moderation" is allowable in either "the tender loves of Romeo and Juliet" or "in the attrocious ambition of Lady Macbeth" (pp. 331–34 [3. 1. 17–21]). Malignity itself is not a sublime passion, but it is likely to be an energetic one. Sublime sentiments arise from sharing the energy, not the malignity, of passion. When we encounter Shylock, we do not join in his "disgusting" hatred or in the fear it may instill in other characters; but, recognizing his capability of hurting or destroying, we respond with a feeling of power (pp. 334–35, 364 [3. 1. 21, 51]). Sublimity may be bestowed by "tyrants" as well as "philosophers"; but although sublimity reaches its height when the requisite energy is displayed along with "amiable and beneficent qualities," in art as in nature "the noxious and destructive powers are more vigorous and energetic in their operations than those of beneficence and preservation." Hence the pleasures of tragedy usually arise from energies displayed in "bad" rather than in "good" actions (pp. 361, 383 [3. 1. 46, 73]).

The empathic sharing of these energies is pleasant in itself and not by virtue of any sort of moral force. By keeping sympathy as the sole basis for tragic pleasure, Knight stays within the affective hypothesis; but he has discarded, along with feelings of pity and fear, the moral direction that these feelings were often supposed to lend to tragedy. The feelings of power that, in Knight's analysis, replace pity and fear as the pleasant emotions of tragedy do not necessarily carry any moral weight. Regarding the moral thrust of tragedy, Knight breaks with both the fabulist hypothesis and the usual version of the affective hypothesis. No one, he says, ever goes to the theater for moral instruction (p. 422 [3. 2. 14]). Knowing that he is only watching actors and actresses appearing as fictitious characters in fictitious events, the spectator would be out of his senses if he considered either characters or events "as real examples, which he is to apply as rules for his own morals" (p. 342–43 [3. 1. 28]). The energies that promote morality and justice are the energies of reason, but these are among the least likely to arouse our interest or awaken our sympathies (pp. 337–41 [3. 1. 25–28]).[7] For interest and sympathy, Knight compares the conspirators in *Venice Preserved* with those in *Julius Caesar*:

> . . . though Shakspeare's poetry rises far above Otway's the gallant and profligate impetuosity of Pierre; and the various conflicting passions of his perfidious friend, are far more interesting and impressive, than the republican firmness of Cassius, or the philosophical benevolence of Brutus; merely because they are more energetic: for it is with the general energy, and not with the particular passions, that we sympathize. *Men fit to disturb the peace of all the world, and rule it when 'tis wildest,* are the proper materials for tragedy; since, how much soever we may dread, or abhor them in reality, we are always delighted with them in fiction. (Pp. 353–54 [3. 1. 39])

Although Knight does not deny that poetry can do some

moral good by diverting man from sensual or violent pleasures to intellectual ones (p. 454 [3. 3. 28]), the energetic delight that he attributes to *Venice Preserved* is not in moral improvement—that is, in cherishing *"mild and benevolent passions"* and subduing *"violent, sordid or selfish"* ones (p. 234 [2. 2. 112]). On the other hand, tragedy does not encourage immorality. It neither redeems nor corrupts. Even though the poet *"throws the veil of magnanimity"* around destructive *"passions and vices,"* he does not make actual crime any less disgusting. "By giving supernatural force and energy to every image and expression, [the pomp of verse and splendor of eloquence] tend to raise the mind above the contemplation of ordinary nature, instead of sinking it to a level with it" (pp. 342 [3. 1. 28]). The causes that combine to infuse the audience with feelings of power are so remote from anything in actual life that, unless the audience is already tainted, it will not be tempted to match these feelings by committing some crime (p. 452 [3. 3. 26]).

Materials that would be unpleasant and even dangerous in actual life are not morally or aesthetically troublesome because the tragic poet "seizes only the energetic qualities and expressions, which he heightens and embellishes, and suppresses the rest . . . as far as the limits of truth in imitation will allow" (pp. 384–85 [3. 1. 75]). This formula for overcoming the disagreeables recalls Knight's definition of "visible beauty" developed in Part 1 of the *Analytical Inquiry*. Visible beauty depends not at all, as Burke believed, on smoothness but only on "irritation" of the eye by "harmonious, but yet brilliant and contrasted combinations of light, shade, and colour" (pp. 57, 60–61, 65, 68 [1. 5. 1, 6, 7, 11, 16]). Therefore, an imitation of objects disgusting and abhorrent in actual life may be pleasing because visible beauty, which makes its impact directly on the eye through light and color, dissociates itself from offensive nonvisual qualities. Perceiving only the visible qualities of an object, the mind takes pleasure in "harmonious and brilliant combinations of tints" even when a painting represents decayed trees, rotten thatch, or a fish market. Since the aesthetic experience comes directly through the senses, the mind is not disturbed by unpleasant associations (pp. 70–72 [1. 5. 18–20]). Just as a painting restricts perception to visual effects that are in themselves pleasing, so does tragedy restrict sympathy to sharing the energy and decision of malignant passions but not the malignant passions themselves. Or, in other words, just as the visual limitations of painting exclude the nonvisible disagreeables, so do the moral limitations of the theater preclude any corruption by evil actions.

Knight separates both visible beauty and the pleasures of tragedy from the *process* of association. The organization of the *Analytical Inquiry* puts sensation, association, and passion in separate compartments. It is not that Knight denies the importance of sensation to association or that of association to sublime passion. In fact, since the eye is affected directly only by light and color, Knight cannot trace sublimity to direct sensation. Sublime passion requires all three kinds of association that Knight explains in Part 2. The first of these Knight calls "improved perception." This results when the mind automatically applies habitual knowledge to recognize sense impressions as signs either of qualities directly apprehended by other senses or of nonsensory qualities. The sense of sight, for instance, has been instructed by the sense of touch to discover "projection" and by experience with paintings to recognize technical competence (pp. 57–58, 102–103 [1. 5. 2–3; 2. 1. 5]). A second kind of association, treated under the heading of "imagination," is that which extends trains of ideas. At the beginning of the *Analytical Inquiry* Knight acknowledges that in its general use "the Greek word *idea*" offers difficulties, being used "sometimes in its proper sense to signify a mental image or vision, and sometimes in others the most adverse and remote, to signify *perception, remembrance, notion, knowledge,* and almost every other operation, or result of operation, of which the mind is capable" (p. 39 [1. 3. 11]). In describing the mind's associating powers, Knight uses the word *idea* in its broader sense. His trains include both "thought and imagery" (p. 136 [2. 2. 1]). As the mind is more richly stored with association, "all the pleasures of the intellect" are increased. "Almost every object of nature or art" is viewed with greater pleasure as it excites "fresh trains and combinations of ideas." These trains, by drawing on established patterns of association, relate each part of an object to the whole and the whole object to others of the same or different kinds (pp. 143–44 [2. 2. 12]). This process increases the enjoyment of works of both nature and art (p. 153 [2. 2. 25]). Since much of the pleasure received from painting, sculpture, music, and poetry "arises from our associating other ideas with those immediately excited by them, . . . the . . . productions of these arts are never thoroughly enjoyed but by persons, whose minds are enriched by a variety of kindred and corresponding imagery." This pleasure extends not only to artistic productions but also "to every object in nature or circumstance in society, that is at all connected with them." Such objects and circumstances are called *picturesque*, because the viewer's pleasures depend to such a large degree on his acquaintance with the art of painting (pp. 145–46 [2. 2. 14–15]).

The third kind of association is that needed by judgment. Judgment is "reasoning from cause and effect, or from analogy or similitude"; it is not so much a kind of reason as "the decision, which reason draws from comparison." It does not admit of absolute demonstration, which is possible only in relations of number and quantity, but must rely on the "habitual association of ideas, and consequently can amount to no more than this; that the thing appears so to us, because it has always appeared so." Syllogistic reasoning has "little or nothing to do with taste; for taste depends upon feeling and sentiment, and not upon demonstration or argument" (pp. 259–60 [2. 3. 1–3]); but judgment, which recognizes order in art and nature not by demonstration but by habitual association, is essential to taste. In poetry it becomes the arbiter of "poetical probability." As long as the actions in a poetic narrative are not demonstrably false—that is, involving inconsistencies in number and quantity—we accept them as "poetically probable" if they "are such as the men, there described, could have produced, had such men ever existed" (pp. 265, 270 [2. 2. 10, 16]). Thus judgment, unlike syllogistic reasoning, has a great deal to do with "feeling and sentiment," for it links passion and event. To be well unified, a tragedy has only to keep the interest centered on those energetic passions that arouse feelings of sublimity. The only essential unity for either tragedy or epic, Knight believes, is the unity of "subject," e.g., "the *ambition of Lady Macbeth*" or "*the anger of Achilles.*" When the actions, no matter how subordinate or episodic, all spring from one subject in a poetically probable succession, "the sentiments of sympathy, which they excite, will all verge on one centre, and be connected by one chain" (pp. 270–75 [2. 3. 17, 19–24]). The chain is forged by the imagination and tested by judgment, which, conditioned by experience with cause and effect, accepts as probable the linking among actions, characters, sentiments, and language.

The emotion of sublimity requires, in addition to direct sensation, these three kinds of association. "Improved perception," for instance, is needed to give the feeling of distance and hence of size. When an object is not sublime by virtue of its physical size, the second kind of association comes into use—that is, trains of ideas must lead to sublimity by linking that object with great size, great exertion, great power, etc. Furthermore, a sublime object must be grasped as a whole, and to establish its oneness, Knight requires the third use of association.

Although dependent for its sublimity on association, the sublime "object" nevertheless stands apart as a kind of end-product of the associating process itself, with pleasures distinguishable from those offered by that process. The pleasures of association are many. They include even the purest and "most permanent" of all gratifications, the attainment of knowledge (p. 458 [3. 3. 33]). Knight allows association a partnership with judgment and, therefore, a contribution to kinds of knowledge not involving number and quantity. But when sublime passions "expand and elevate the mind" (p. 333 [3. 1. 19]), what enlarges the mind is not the fusion of knowledge with sensation. Instead, the expanding force is the "simple," intuited idea which association has arrived at. The audience "delights in [the] unity and simplicity of [a tragic] character" (p. 411 [3. 2. 2]). Macbeth is "an ungrateful traitor, murderer, usurper, and tyrant . . . made, in the highest degree, interesting, by . . . sublime flashes of generosity, magnanimity, courage, and tenderness" (p. 352 [3. 1. 38]). Such a diverse and complicated character attains "simplicity" only if the judgment accepts the coherence of the character's diverse emotions. Poetical probability, based on a network of habitual associations, so links Macbeth's words and actions with each other and with the other events in the play that the audience's "sentiments of sympathy" converge to one energetic center. In defining simplicity, Knight pays his respects to the visible sublime. Objects represented in sublime poetry should be *"distinct* without being *determinate"* (p. 388 [3. 1. 81]).[8] The images should be individually clear, but the quantitative limits of an object should be left to the imagination. In its concern for visible extension, Knight's reluctance to specify sublime dimensions recalls not only Burke's predilection for "obscurity" (which Knight chooses to reject as implying the "indistinct" rather than the indeterminate) but also earlier admonitions, like Baillie's *(Essay on the Sublime,* p. 9), that too much attention to detail will violate "simplicity" and frustrate the soul's quickness in multiplication: "In grasping at infinity," says Knight, "the mind exercises the powers . . . of multiplying without end" (pp. 361–62 [3. 1. 47]). The expansion of the mind resulting from sympathetic feelings of power is analogous to that attained by "contemplating all vast and immense objects" or objects to which association has given the emotional equivalence of vastness (p. 362 [3. 1. 48]). This expansion is not in the associational linking but in the empathic response to the resulting idea. In tragedy the mind expands itself, not by comprehending in some large design the tragic character's thought and feeling, but by trying to share the energy of that thought and feeling. When it comes to sublimity, Knight values the "strength of reasoning" of Achilles, Macbeth, and Othello for the vigor it gives the expression of passion, and not for its organization of experience in the face of evil (pp. 395–96 [3. 1. 85]). Sublime mental expansion will be promoted as additional associations—of Macbeth, for example, with further instances of ambition, murder, and marital love —build up the idea of energy that the mind must try to comprehend; but while it is the role of imagination to increase the size of "its conceptions . . . to the utmost verge of probability" (p. 389 [3. 1. 81]), it is not association itself that extends the mind toward sublimity, but the mind's effort to grasp the ever-expanding conception of energy which associations lead to.

After the chapter "Of the Sublime and Pathetic," the *Analytical Inquiry* ends with two much shorter chapters: "Of the Ridiculous" and "Of Novelty." The ridiculous is "diametrically opposite to the sublime and pathetic . . .: for laughter is an expression of joy and exultation" arising "not from sympathy but triumph." It does not heighten and embellish "the general energies of human nature" but exposes and exaggerates "its particular weaknesses and defects." The passions of tragedy converge in an elevating "simplicity" of character, whereas the detachment of comedy assembles "incongruities and inconsistencies" of character to pervert or degrade "the natural character of man" (pp. 410–11 [3. 2. 1–2]). For any moral effect, Knight is as dubious of comedy as of tragedy. In the latter case, the audience attends the theater "merely to sympathize with the general energies" and, in the former, "to laugh at the particular weaknesses of human nature." Both tragedy and comedy must depart from "the common prudence" that the audience knows in its domestic life (p. 422 [3. 2. 14–15]). The pleasure of the audience, like all pleasure, requires "novelty," the subject of Knight's closing chapter. Pleasure does not lie in gratified desires or in satisfied curiosity. Even knowledge, although its acquirement outlasts other pleasures, eventually "ceases to charm" (pp. 458–59 [3. 3. 32–33]). Man's "real happiness consists in the *means,* and not in the *end*:—in *acquisition,* and not in *possession*." Novelty lies in "new ideas," in "new trains of thought," in the "renewal and extension of affections and atttachments," in "new circumstances and situations" and "the new lights, in which we . . . view them," in "new exertions and variations of pursuit," and, above all, in "the unlimited power of fancy" to multiply and vary "the objects, the results, and the gratifications of our pursuits beyond the bounds of reality, or probable duration of existence" (p. 469 [3. 3. 40]). In this chapter Knight does not mention sublimity, and he speaks of tragedy only to elaborate what he has already said about its amorality (p. 450–51 [3. 3. 25]); but, of course, it is against a dying life of satisfied desire that a tragic character directs his sublime energy. To share this energy, if not its specific goals, seemed to Knight an important and elevating pleasure. Sublimity could still be relied on to relieve indolence and languor.

3

For good sense, urbanity, dramatic insight, and ease and clarity of style, Knight is one of the most attractive writers in this study. If Alison is disappointingly reactionary in his practical criticism, Knight is pleasingly liberal. Alison, although arguing for unity of emotion or "character" as the essential one in tragedy, scolds Shakespeare for multiple plotting and turns to the classical structure of Corneille to bring all the parts of a tragedy into emotional focus. Knight believes that the interest in tragedy must center on those energetic passions that give rise to sublimity, and to gain this concentration he requires only a "unity of subject" from which all events are chained by "poetical probability." As in *Macbeth*, there may be more than one principal action in addition to a variety of subordinate actions. When it comes to explaining the evil characters in tragedy, Knight is consistent in a way that Alison is not. For Knight, malignant characters are the usual source of those energetic passions which tragedy demands. Alison, on the other hand, although he finds association capable of making the physically ugly become agreeable, justifies ugly characters because by contrast they highlight the beauty of virtuous ones. Alison scarcely does justice to Iago or Richard III, and, besides, he would condemn to displeasure plays in which the characters are mainly or entirely malignant (a kind of play which, to be sure, has become more common since Alison's time).

Nevertheless, Knight's aesthetic is psychologically a step backward from Alison's. Knight is still a follower of Addison, Baillie, and especially Burke in ways that make him less representative of Romantic criticism than Alison. Knight is unlike Burke in that he distinguishes aesthetic from practical experience, finds pleasure in sympathy with power rather than in sympathy with suffering and fear, rejects any moral thrust of tragic sympathy, and cannot attribute sublimity to direct sensation. But, although he makes the associating power of the imagination necessary to the sublime, Knight is like Baillie and Burke in separating association (the process) from the sublimity of passion (the result of that process). Sublime expansion is a matter, not of adding trains of ideas, but of trying to comprehend, empathically, the physical size of an object or more frequently to grasp its equivalent in energy or power.

Knowledge brought by association into a complex of ideas and the resulting organization of human experience may be necessary to, but it is not a part of, the aesthetic experience that Knight calls sublime. Awareness that a character represents the power to hurt or destroy is needed if one is sympathetically to acquire through that character a feeling of power; but the ultimate pleasure lies in this feeling itself and not in discovering how this evil character in his, or in any other, version of reality balances the forces of good and evil. For Knight, the power bestowed by tragedy comes from sharing the energy or power of certain feelings. For Hazlitt, a decade later, this power comes both from feeling and from knowing, as these powers of the mind are united by the imagination. This is not to deny that Knight's shared feeling of power is important among the pleasures of tragedy. It undoubtedly is. But by tracing sublime emotion to the whole process of association Hazlitt gives tragic pleasure a deeper penetration.

CHAPTER SEVEN

THE SUBLIME OF VISION

Romantic poets and critics found sublimity in the process of perception rather than in unique qualities of external objects. This process draws on all the mind's resources of sensation, thought, and feeling, a combination no longer restricted by intellectual shortcomings attributed to the imagination. Romantic poetry did not abandon big mountains and overtly passionate characters, but a small flower or an old Cumberland beggar might assert an equal claim to sublimity. The fullness of the imaginative process became more important to the sublime than visible size or the duplication of its emotional impact.

Despite the Romantic poets' use of concrete particulars to stimulate the imagination, the Romantic conceptions of both beauty and sublimity repudiate the merely visual. In itself the visual represents a defective kind of reality which is made whole only as the full power of the mind is brought to bear on it. Both beauty and sublimity require the laws of the mind to organize the phenomena of the senses. When Blake's grain of sand becomes the world or his "round disk" of a sun grows into an "Innumerable company of the Heav-

enly host,"[1] the imagination has not duplicated and redupli-
cated the visual but has constructed a version of reality in
which the original image has been transmuted by the power
of thought. For Wordsworth, when he saw the "unveiled
summit of Mont Blanc" and even after Simplon's "steep and
rugged road" had led him successfully across the Alps, he felt
only desolation. It was fourteen years later—the "light of
sense" having gone out, but "with a flash that . . . recalled /
The invisible world"—that his imagination lighted up the
mountains with his reason for having sought them.

> Our destiny, our being's heart and home,
> Is with infinitude, and only there;
> With hope it is, hope that can never die,
> Effort, and expectation, and desire,
> And something evermore about to be.[2]

In this eternal aspiration, Wordsworth finds a greater permanence and glory than even the mountains can lay claim to.
When Coleridge in his imagination gazed on Mont Blanc, the
"silent Mount"—although "still present to the bodily sense"
—vanished from his "thought," and "entranced in prayer /
[he] worshipped the Invisible alone."[3] The power inherent in
Shelley's Mont Blanc acquires its moral direction only from
the "human mind" in its "unremitting interchange" / With
the clear universe of things around." Without this interchange, "silence and solitude" would be only "vacancy."[4]

These examples of the mind stretching out to vision have
not been labeled by these poets as "sublime," although in
Shelley's "Mont Blanc" the speaker, as he muses on the "fan-
tasy" his mind creates, seems "in a trance sublime and
strange" (l. 35). In "Lines Composed a Few Miles above
Tintern Abbey" Wordsworth's "sense sublime / Of something . . . / Whose dwelling is the light of setting suns" unmistakably requires the mind to open from sensation to vision;[5] but the use of the word *sublime* in Romantic poetry,
even in the poets just quoted, cannot be counted on to have
this precise meaning. More important than the word itself is
the conception of psychological size with which Alison in his

definition of sublimity removed the need for visual size or its equivalent. This conception with its resulting sublime of vision is identifiable whether it is named sublime, beautiful, or nothing at all. Fortunately, we have a few definitions to help out.

Blake's "Definition of the Most Sublime Poetry" is "Allegory address'd to the Intellectual powers, while it is altogether hidden from the Corporeal Understanding."[6] In his annotations to Reynolds's *Discourses,* Blake angrily rejects Burke's definitions of the sublime and the beautiful as deferring to the spurious reality of Locke and Newton. He himself places the sublime and the beautiful within a superior reality called "Inspiration and Vision" or, in other words, within the imaginative fusion of the internal and external.[7] Whereas Burke's sublime and beautiful are the abstractions of a divided mind, "Vision" requires all the faculties working together. In *The Marriage of Heaven and Hell* Blake writes: "The head Sublime, the heart Pathos, the genitals Beauty, and the hands & feet Proportion";[8] but these, of course, are distinctions that disappear in the wholeness of a human being or of a work of art. Blake's sublime implies strength, energy, and above all intellectual power. The beauty of a work of art does not stand apart from these qualities, but, rather, it displays them. "The Beauty proper for sublime art is lineaments, or forms and features that are capable of being the receptacles of intellect."[9] As far as Blake's own poetry is concerned, the beautiful is difficult to distinguish from the sublime. Beauty as line and form is evident in Blake's admiration for the naked human body, but beauty, like sublimity, is always visionary. It may be "female," "soft," and "sweet," or "giant," "majestic," "awful," "terrible," and "dreadful."[10] Vision, whether called sublime or beautiful, cannot dispense with the minutely visual. Blake condemns both Reynolds's "general forms" and the obscurity of Burke's sublime as examples of Lockean abstraction. "Broken Colours & Broken Lines & Broken Masses are Equally Subversive of the Sublime," for the sublime always requires "Minute Neatness of Execution." Vision can complete itself only by being "Determinate & Perfect" in its sensory form.[11] This visual firmness of detail is not to be confused with a literal over-explicitness; for the latter inhibits the imagination, while the former is necessary to comprehending "what is grand."[12]

In a passage in *Allsop's Recollections* Coleridge makes the distinction to which—as C. D. Thorpe has pointed out—he seems to hold in several passages on the sublime scattered throughout his work.[13]

THE GRAND AND THE SUBLIME

What can be finer in any poet than that beautiful passage in Milton—

> . . . *Onward he moved*
> *And thousands of his saints around.*

This is grandeur, but it is grandeur without completeness: but he adds—

> *Far off their coming shone;*

which is the highest sublime. There is *total* completeness.

So I would say that the Saviour praying on the Mountain, the Desert on one hand, the Sea on the other, the city at an immense distance below, was sublime. But I should say of the Saviour looking towards the City, his countenance full of pity, that he was majestic, and of the situation that it was grand.

When the whole and the parts are seen at once, as mutually producing and explaining each other, as unity in multeity, there results shapeliness—*forma formosa*. Where the perfection of *form* is combined with pleasurableness in the sensations, excited by the matters or substances so formed, there results the beautiful.

Corollary.—Hence colour is eminently subservient to beauty, because it is susceptible of forms, i.e. outline, and yet is a sensation. But a rich mass of scarlet clouds, seen without any attention to the *form* of the mass or of the parts, may be a *delightful* but not a beautiful object or colour.

When there is a deficiency of unity in the line forming the whole (as angularity, for instance), and of number in the plurality or the parts, there arises the formal.

When the parts are numerous, and impressive, and predominate, so as to prevent or greatly lessen the attention to the whole, there results the grand.

Where the impression of the whole, i.e. the sense of unity, predominates, so as to abstract the mind from the parts—the majestic.

Where the parts by their harmony produce an effect of a whole, but there is no seen form of a whole producing or explaining the parts, i.e. when the parts only are seen and distinguished, but the whole is felt—the picturesque.

Where neither whole nor parts, but unity, as boundless or endless *allness*—the sublime.[14]

The mind, unable to grasp the totality of the image, but nevertheless aware of its unity, experiences the sort of elevating expansion that the sublime had long been noted for. Kant describes, as the first stage of the sublime experience, a baffling inability to grasp the whole object; but he also requires a complementary stage, wherein "the law of reason" asserts its superiority to the imagination "as our highest measure of magnitude." As we thus became aware that all "sensible standards" are an inadequate measure of magnitude, we enjoy "the feeling of . . . [our] supersensible destination."[15] However, Coleridge, who believes that the sublime "suspends the power of comparison," must deny any second step.[16] In fact, he does not need this second step, for the unity which he speaks of implies that reason has already been at work organizing images to mirror its intuition of infinite harmony.

For Coleridge, reason is the organ or faculty through which we perceive the universal and by means of which we organize the phenomenal world. "Unity, as boundless or endless allness," is the unity of universal law, a "whole" which obviously cannot be "seen." In relation to this "whole" the "parts" make a contribution different from the one that visible particulars make to beauty, where the viewer's power of comparison gives visibility to form through the interaction of these particulars. But in sublimity the visible details, while "still present to the bodily sense," become "parts" of an invisible whole and therefore no longer distinguishable by their merely visual lineaments, which as such must "vanish from [the viewer's] thought." An object may be either beautiful or sublime to different people, or even to the same person at different times, but it cannot be both beautiful and sublime to the same person at the same moment.[17] In Coleridge's description of a scene on the Lake at Ratzeburg the visual details "vanish" into a "glory" which appears to be that of the sublime:

> On some of the largest of these islands, the fishermen stood pulling out their immense nets through the holes made in the ice for this purpose, and the men, their net-poles, and their huge nets, were a part of the glory; say rather, it appeared as if the rich crimson light had shaped itself into these forms, figures, and attitudes, to make a glorious vision in mockery of earthly things.[18]

The details of the scene were sharply defined in Coleridge's sight; but as his imagination organized these details according to eternal law, the "forms, figures, and attitudes" were no longer distinguishable as "men, their net poles, and the huge nets" but shaped by "rich crimson light" into "a glorious vision" that mocked earthly things.

Neither Coleridge nor the other Romantic poets meant that a work of art can become sublime only at the expense of visual fidelity. For Coleridge, the suppression of the particular would result in only the "majestic" (Addison's "greatness," or, especially, Baillie's sublime), just as domination by the parts over the whole would produce the "formal," the "grand," or the "picturesque." Coleridge draws on Schlegel's comparison of Greek and Gothic architecture to show the greater scope that the latter gives to the imagination. When he enters a Greek church, his "eye is charmed" and his "mind elated," but on entering a cathedral, he is "lost to the actualities" surrounding him, his "whole being expands to the infinite."[19] For Addison, the bold and rounded forms of classical architecture are grander than a Gothic cathedral because they allow the eye to "surround" some ample form (*S.* 415), whereas for Coleridge the Gothic multiplicity of detail impels the mind beyond visual extension. For the same reason the materials of Greek and Roman mythology seem less suitable for sublime poetry than those of the Christian and

Hebrew religion. The former limit the range of feeling because the imagination has only "definite Forms (i.e. [the gods and goddesses of] the Religion of Greece and Rome)" to "work thro' "; whereas the latter keep the imagination "barren in definite Forms" while, "in cooperation with the Understanding [it] labours after an obscure and indefinite Vastness—this is Christianity."[20] As sublime poetry Wordsworth selects "parts of the Holy Scriptures, . . . the works of Milton; and . . . those of Spenser" in preference to the writings of "ancient Greece and Rome, because the anthropomorphitism of the Pagan religion subjected the minds of the greatest poets in those countries too much to the bondage of definite form."[21] The gods and goddesses of pagan religion are sculptured theology in which, as in many an eighteenth-century sublime "object," the imagination has already completed its major role. But the angels and archangels of Christianity move more powerfully in the wider realms of the imagination, their shapes and activities unconfined by the limitations of the human form.[22] Although the sublime of vision had escaped the limitations of visual size, the religious import of the sublime persisted. The Scriptures and *Paradise Lost* were hard to displace as the sublimest poetry, and supernatural beings often seemed better able than the characters of tragedy to project the mind toward vision.

Wordsworth and Coleridge themselves wrote tragedies, of course, and these tragedies mark one kind of transition from the visible sublime to the sublime of vision. Wordsworth's *The Borderers* (written 1796–97, published 1842) and Coleridge's *Remorse* (written as *Osorio* in 1797, revised and retitled in 1812, produced at Drury Lane in 1813, and published the same year) center on the theme of remorse.[23] Both plays use the paraphernalia of Gothicism. Their ruined castles, stormy nights, wild and rocky landscapes, moldering dungeons, and solitary chapels recall many Gothic dramas and, ultimately, Burke's sublime of terror. Remorse, a stock passion of Gothic villains and heroes, was conventionally morbid and frightening, a tormented conscience being the equivalent in terrible effects to storms and dungeons.[24] In

The Borderers and *Remorse*, however, Wordsworth and Coleridge build remorse into a more comprehensive version of reality, in which the Gothic details stimulate thought as well as feeling. The resulting "vision" transcends the palpable horrors, not with the vague suggestions of the supernatural that often characterize the Gothic, but with an exploration of the human mind for good and evil.

The Borderers dramatizes what Wordsworth considered to be shortcomings of Godwin's *Political Justice.* It is visionary not only in molding sensory details to reflect moral qualities but in repudiating the fractioned mind implicit in Locke's and Godwin's conception of reason. As in other Gothic dramas, the principal characters are outlaws uncontrolled by "established Law and Government," but here there is a philosophic reason for their freedom: they are "at liberty to act on their own impulses" without any possible corruption by manmade institutions (1:342).[25] To this extent, then, Wordsworth is meeting Godwin on his own ground. Wordworth's purpose is to move and instruct the reader "by lights penetrating somewhat into the depth of our nature" (1:342). The two characters whose minds are probed to their depths are Marmaduke and Oswald. Marmaduke, the leader of a band of outlaws dedicated to helping the weak against their oppressors, stands for benevolence. He is, according to Oswald, a "fool of feeling" (act 2, l. 558). Oswald, another outlaw but a decidedly more intricate character, is "a young man of great intellectual powers yet without any solid principles of genuine benevolence. His master passions are pride and the love of distinction" (1:345). Like other Gothic protagonists he has committed a great crime; but unremorseful, he plans and carries out additional crimes in order to maintain the selfish pride "which made the first crime attractive." Oswald's devotion to his own cunning approaches superstition in the "sacred importance" he attaches to his "vicious purposes" (1:348). He even supports his pride with a belief in spirits (act 5, ll. 1440–47). His moral anarchy is appropriately imaged in Gothic gloom and violence as he derides Marmaduke for serving "peace and order": ". . . it is / In darkness and in tempest that we seek / The majesty of him who rules the world" (act 2, ll. 614–17). Oswald is a more extreme case than any considered in *Political Justice*, but Wordsworth's allusions to Godwinian reason are unmistakable. Godwin, of course, had assumed an identity of interests, discoverable by reason, as a basis for equating self-interest with benevolence; but Wordsworth wished to show that reason divorced from benevolence to serve pride is only destructive. In order to corrupt Marmaduke into a moral replica of himself, Oswald devises an elaborate set of lies to provoke Marmaduke into deserting Idonea, the woman he loves, and murdering her father, Herbert. Plunged by his suspicions into Oswald's world of horror, Marmaduke nevertheless puts Oswald's powers of invention to a severe test before he finally succumbs. He stops short of actually stabbing Herbert but leaves him on a stormy heath to die. When, having found out Oswald's lies, he returns to save the old man, it is too late. Unfit, as her father's murderer, to remain in Idonea's company or in that of any other decent person, Marmaduke embarks on a wandering life of penance; while Oswald, still unrepentant in his pride, is stabbed to death by one of the good outlaws. His melodramatic death is less important to the tragedy than his obdurate remorselessness. In contrast to the natural forms in "Tintern Abbey" and "The Prelude," those perceived by Oswald have merely served the ego. When, he says, he

> surveyed
> The moonlight desert, and the moonlight sea:
> In these my lonely wanderings I perceived
> What mighty objects do impress their forms
> To elevate our intellectual being;
> And felt, if aught deserves a curse,
> 'Tis that worst principle of ill which dooms
> A thing so great to perish self-consumed.
> —So much for my remorse! (Act. 4, ll. 1806–17)

Like other "mighty objects" we have encountered in descriptions of the sublime, these forms enhance the viewer's opinion of himself; but Wordsworth would not have called them sublime, for—perceived by a mind which, although strong in intellect, is defective in compassion—they have reflected only a self-centered pride.[26]

As its twenty-night run at Drury Lane attests, *Remorse* shows considerable dramatic skill. Whereas in *The Borderers* the scenes shift in confusion with little in the way of action to tie them together, Coleridge manages to keep an equally preposterous series of events intelligible and, despite a good deal of psychological analysis at critical moments, emotionally sustained. Samuel C. Chew has described Coleridge's plays—along with those of Joanna Baillie, Byron, and Browning—as substituting "spiritual for external action" and revealing "an increasing interest in the psychology of situation, a growing inattention to mere plot, a new and (judging by old standards) disproportionate insistence upon motive."[27] In *Remorse* the psychology of situation is less complex and, I think, less interesting than in *The Borderers*; but again it shows the author using Gothic details to serve the sublime of vision. And again, the principal tension is between the man of benevolence and the man whose intellect serves only his selfish pride. Alvar is the benevolent elder son of Marquis Valdez; Ordonio is the scheming younger son, who, believing that he has disposed of Alvar at the hands of a paid assassin, wants to marry Teresa, Alvar's betrothed. Returning in disguise from his supposed grave, Alvar is determined, not to avenge himself, but to make Ordonio capable of true remorse. Early in Act 1, Zulimez, Alvar's attendant, distinguishes between two kinds of remorse, with imagery appropriate to each kind:

> Remorse is as the heart in which it grows:
> If that be gentle, it drops balmy dews
> Of true repentance; but if proud and gloomy,
> It is a poison-tree, that pierced to the inmost
> Weeps only tears of poison! (1. 1. 20–24)[28]

The "proud and gloomy" kind of remorse is that which, running through many Gothic novels and plays, reached a consummation in Byron's *Manfred*. Alvar, the victim of lies as well as attempted murder, had at first wanted his enemies to suffer the remorse that "clings with poisonous tooth, inextricable / As the gored lion's bite (1. 2. 311–12), until, his benevolence having overcome his vengefulness, he calls Nature to his brother's aid with "soft influences, / . . . sunny hues, fair forms, and breathing sweets" (5. 1. 22–23). But Ordonio, a "blind self-worshipper" (5. 1. 157) like Wordsworth's Oswald, finds only disorder in nature: "this same world of ours, / 'Tis but a pool amidst a storm of rain" (5. 1. 112). Again like Oswald, he believes in spirits (2. 2. 144; 3. 1. 22)[29]—a superstition, rejected by Alvar and Teresa, that makes Ordonio all the readier to believe in the "wandering demons" that Alvar supposedly conjures up to disclose the attempt on his life (3. 1. 134ff). Yet when, after descending into a dungeon to kill the imprisoned Alvar, Ordonio realizes his brother's unshaken love, he humbles himself and asks forgiveness—before he is knifed by the widow of another of his victims. Perhaps because of the exigencies of stage production, Ordonio's last moments have been made more Gothic and melodramatic than those of the earlier Osorio, but in both versions of the play Coleridge's interest is clearly to show that the villain has lost his "blind self-worship" in contrition. Perhaps it would be going too far to conclude that all the Gothic imagery bears on Coleridge's definition of remorse. Nevertheless the imagery often supports the conclusion that the phenomenal world, seen through a mind fragmented by selfish pride, shows only painful disorder, which yields to order as the mind regains its wholeness.

Coleridge does not call Alvar's—or his own—vision in *Remorse* "sublime." He does use the word "sublime," however, to describe the reach of imagination in Shakespearean tragedy. Objecting to Schiller's "mere material sublime," Coleridge cites Shakespeare's more powerful and genuine sublimity attained without recourse to physically large objects: "Schiller . . . sets you a whole town on fire, and throws infants with their mothers into flames, or locks up a father in an old tower. But Shakespeare drops a handkerchief, and the same or greater effects follow."[30] Coleridge nevertheless turns to the Hebrew Scriptures and to Milton for his examples of the greatest sublimity.[31] Wordsworth, as we have seen, did not include among the most sublime poets either Shakespeare or any other dramatic poet. Wordsworth measured the greatest poetry by its sublimity, usually equating the sublime with imagination and leaving beauty to fancy.[32] For Wordsworth, as for Dennis, the religious force of the sublime seems to be the principal reason for locating the sublime in other genres than tragedy. In his 1815 Preface, Wordsworth designates as the highest poetry "the grand store-house of enthusiastic and meditative Imagination."[33] James Scoggins has shown Wordsworth's indebtedness to Coleridge and, through Coleridge to Kant, for his view of the sublime;[34] but the passage quoted above, it would seem, also reflects Dennis's distinction between "Enthusiastick Passions" and "Vulgar Passions," which are moved, respectively, by "Ideas in Contemplation, or the Meditation of things that belong not to common Life" (i.e., especially, religious ideas) and by "Objects themselves, or by the Ideas in the ordinary Course of Life."[35] Enthusiastic passions, says Dennis, prevail "in those parts of Epick Poetry, where the Poet speaks himself, or the Eldest of the Muses for him, [and] in the greater Ode"; whereas the vulgar passions "prevail in those parts of an Epick and Dramatick Poem, where the Poet introduces Persons holding Conversation together."[36] This latter category, of course, includes tragedy. Wordsworth's statement in his 1815 Preface and his examples in that essay strongly suggest that he, too, would exclude tragedy from the highest reaches of sublimity.[37]

Like Coleridge and Wordsworth, De Quincey analyzes the sublime in some detail and finds it consummated in the nondramatic.[38] For De Quincey, as for Coleridge, beauty and sublimity are mutually exclusive. De Quincey identifies the sublime—whether "moral," "ethicophysical," or "dark"—with the infinite or the mysterious, and, ultimately, with the religious. He does not go as far as Coleridge in excluding Greek poetry from sublimity; but in describing the ethicophysical sublime—which displays great moral energy against a physically vast background—his essay "On Milton" (1839) recognizes "but one great model surviving in the Greek poetry: viz. the gigantic drama of the Prometheus crucified on Mount Elborus."[39] De Quincey traces the moral sublime—which evidently arises from a realization of man's essential dignity—back to Roman literature, where this quality is exhibited in a manner "perfectly distinct from anything known to the Greek poetry." De Quincey makes Milton his principal example of the highest sublimity. "In Milton only, first and last, is the power of the sublime revealed. In Milton only does this great agency blaze and glow as a furnace kept up to a white heat, without suspicion of collapse."[40] The "dark sublime," which is both mysterious and dreadful, is likewise found in Milton.[41] De Quincey also refers, on one occasion, to "the sublimities of earthly misery and of human frenzy," as seen in Shakespeare, but the whole passage makes it clear that he finds "the solemn wheelings of the Miltonic movement" more sublime.[42]

The sublime that was religious was the sublime more likely to remain distinct from beauty. In Blake and Shelley, the sublime at its highest reach is not confined to the Scriptures and the epic. Blake, to be sure, finds sublimity in the Bible[43] and in his own prophetic poetry,[44] in which the influences of the Bible and Milton are strong. But he also finds it in *The Canterbury Tales*. Here the characters are living people in whose description Chaucer is "minute and exact," yet their sublimity cannot be disputed.[45] As unsurpassable examples of "Inspiration"—and presumably the sublime of vision—Blake lists "Milton, Shakspeare, Michael Angelo, Raphael, the finest specimens of Ancient Sculpture and Painting and Architecture, Gothic, Grecian, Hindoo, and Egyptian." These represent "the extent of the human mind."[46] Although Shakespeare became his guide "in riper years,"[47] Blake does not describe tragedy as sublime or beautiful. In fact, he mentions tragedy or the tragic only three times, twice in admiration of Chaucer's Monk and the Monk's definition of tragedy as a fall from prosperity to misery.[48] In *Jerusalem* Blake disparages the moral delights that, we have seen, were accorded tragedy by Burke and his followers: ". . . pitying & weeping as at a trajic scene / The soul drinks murder & revenge & applauds its own holiness."[49] As Northrop Frye points out, "Blake's complete vision is a divine comedy"; the "more profound" a tragedy is, "the more readily it leads to a resurrection of the imagination in the spectators."[50] If Blake admired Shakespeare's tragedies, as he evidently did, it was because he found in them the mental dimensions that vision demands.

For Shelley, beauty is the eternal order of the universe comprehended through the poet's participation in "the eternal, the infinite, and the one" beyond the limits of "time and place."[51] Thus Shelley expands beauty to the limits of Coleridge's sublimity, beyond which there is hardly any place for the imagination to go. Shelley also uses the word *sublime* to describe great poetry, but it can only mean beauty of a certain kind (grand, awe-inspiring, elevated) or remarkable success in attaining beauty. To project the mind toward the eternal and the infinite he on occasion uses mythic beings, personifications rather than persons, but within the confines of the stage he also finds resources to express "the beautiful and the true."[52] Truth is eternal order, beauty is its reflection in art, and goodness its expression in conduct.[53] Morality and beauty have identical origins, therefore, in a mind that matches the everlasting order of things. In bringing the mind into some sort of harmony, tragedy has been the most widely successful of all poetic genres.

The prefaces to *Prometheus Unbound* and *The Cenci* recall Dennis's distinction between works addressed to the "enthusiastick" and the "vulgar" passions. In *Prometheus Unbound* Shelley proposes "to familiarize the highly refined imagination of the more select classes of poetical readers with beautiful idealisms of moral excellence; aware that until the mind can love, and admire, and trust, and hope, and endure, reasoned principles of moral conduct are seeds cast upon the highway of life which the unconscious passenger tramples into dust."[54] However, in *The Cenci* (written in 1819 after Act III of *Prometheus Unbound*) Shelley proposes to deal only with "a sad reality,"[55] idealized to the extent that the pleasure arising from the poetry may mitigate "the actual horror of the events"[56] but not to the degree that would keep it from "the multitude."[57] Without forgetting that in dramatic composition imagery must be "reserved simply for the full development and illustration" of passion, Shelley has written "without an over-fastidiousness and learned choice of words." But if he has been more careful to use "the familiar language of men," he has not abridged his moral purpose, which is to teach "the human heart, through its sympathies and antipathies, the knowledge of itself; in proportion to the possession of which knowledge, every human being is wise, just, sincere, tolerant, and kind."[58] To use Dennis's words comparing tragedy with the epic, Shelley believed that *The Cenci* would "please and instruct more generally"[59] than *Prometheus Unbound*; but unlike Dennis he did not hold tragedy incapable of arousing the most elevated passions.

As far as the breadth of moral effectiveness is concerned, Shelley in *A Defence of Poetry* gives tragedy a higher place than any other kind of poetry. The power of drama to enlarge the imagination makes the "connexion of poetry and social good . . . more observable in the drama than in whatever other form" as evident in continued correspondence of "the highest perfection of human society . . . with the highest dramatic excellence."[60] The drama reached its greatest power in Athens, for "the Athenians employed language, action, music, painting, the dance, and religious institutions" to support each other in a "beautiful proportion and unity." Modern drama is defective in the resources assembled by Greek tragedy, but nevertheless "*King Lear* . . . may be judged to be the most perfect specimen of the dramatic art existing in the world."[61] In the Preface to *The Cenci* Shelley calls tragedy the "highest species of the drama" and, as "the deepest and the sublimest tragic compositions," cites "*King Lear,* and the two plays in which the tale of Ædipus is told."[62]

Like Dennis's "enthusiasm," the beauty and sublimity that Shelley finds in tragedy requires mental expansion initiated by imagery and harmonizing the whole mind in a moment of moral insight; but for Shelley this insight calls for penetrating man's inner nature rather than comprehending

111

some extrahuman authority through its manipulation of human affairs.[63] This penetration is achieved as sympathy extends the scope of the imagination.

> The imagination is enlarged by a sympathy with pains and passions so mighty, that they distend in their conception the capacity of that by which they are conceived; the good affections are strengthened by pity, indignation, terror and sorrow; and an exalted calm is prolonged from the satiety of this high exercise of them into the tumult of familiar life: even crime is disarmed of half its horror and all its contagion by being represented as the fatal consequence of the unfathomable agencies of nature; error is thus divested of its wilfulness; men can no longer cherish it as the creation of their choice. In a drama of the highest order there is little food for censure or hatred; it teaches rather self-knowledge and self-respect. Neither the eye nor the mind can see itself, unless reflected upon that which it resembles.[64]

Sympathetic identification extends our capacity to share the feelings of others and therefore to become less selfish; but if we are to disarm crime of half its horror and divest error of its wilfulness, our sympathetic identification must extend itself to sharing both the character's and the poet's thoughts— not merely by following the sequence of motives and actions but also by comprehending the balance of good and evil within a character and hence within ourselves. In both *Prometheus Unbound* and *The Cenci* Shelley portrays man as not innately evil but so flawed that some weakness of will or error in judgment will commit him to an evil act (revenge, for instance) and its necessary chain of consequences. This chain can be broken only if the original cause of evil is removed (hate, for example, giving way to love). In *The Cenci*, after Beatrice has been violated by her father, her impatience for revenge precipitates a necessary chain of events: the involvement of other characters, the hiring of assassins, the murder of Count Cenci, and finally the trial and execution of Beatrice. Yet, despite her complicity, Beatrice maintains that she, "Though wrapped in a strange cloud of crime and shame / Lived ever holy and unstained" (act 5, sc. 4, ll. 148–

49). Other characters, both before and after the murder, assert her innocence with images of "bright loveliness" in a "dark world" (4. 1. 121–22). If, as Shelley says in the Preface, imagery is the "flesh" which the imagination assumes for "the redemption of human passion," Beatrice as well as her passion is redeemed. Her crime is duly punished; yet, once Beatrice had become vengefully impatient, her crime was "divested of its wilfulness," and, by her conviction of an innate innocence which may be regained through gentleness and tears and patience (5. 1. 143–45), it has been "disarmed of half its horror."[65] In *The Cenci* the "enlargement of the imagination" that Shelley claims for tragedy has reached from concrete particulars into vision, wherein good and evil are defined, not by external authority, but by the human mind as it tries to organize a world of pain.

Blake, Coleridge, Wordsworth, De Quincey, and Shelley have all followed the example of Alison in breaking the sublime free from visual extension. So has Leigh Hunt, who in 1844 synthesized a number of Romantic views on the imagination in "An Answer to the Question What is Poetry?" Hunt selects, as showing an imaginative fusion of the physical and the moral, "Antony's likening his changing fortunes to the cloud-rack; Lear's appeal to the old age of the heavens; Satan's appearance in the horizon, like a fleet 'hanging in the clouds';" and Shelley's " 'dome of many-coloured glass.' " These images are all visionary. They all carry some suggestion of physical size, to be sure, but the "vastness" which Hunt attributes to them lies principally in the "weight of thought and feeling" which, along with "freedom from visibility," distinguishes imagination from fancy.[66]

The religious implications of the sublime, a vestige of its history, sometimes continued to exclude the dramatic from the greatest sublimity; but nevertheless tragedy was admitted to the sublime of vision and sometimes, as in Shelley, considered as sublime as any other genre. Hunt also found the imagination consummating its power of expansion in tragedy as well as in other "serious" poetry and achieving an identity of truth and beauty which "draws [pleasure] out of pain."[67]

Hunt's analysis of this process, however, is relatively slight. For the most thorough application of Alison's psychology to tragedy and for the elevation of tragedy to a sublimity surpassing that of any other kind of poetry, we must look at Hazlitt and Keats.

CHAPTER EIGHT

HAZLITT

For Alison, the imagination assimilates the findings of reason, while intense feeling draws all the resources of the mind into the creative act; but Alison did not allow his trains of ideas to bring the greatest of tragic disagreeables, human evil, into the pleasant light of knowledge. His trains could draw off the pain from physical, but not from moral, ugliness. Alison, despite the subjectivity of his aesthetic, apparently deferred to extrahuman authority to make evil bearable in ways not specified in his analysis of tragedy. The sublime of vision puts reality and the authority for organizing it inside the mind. Where or how that authority is derived is a matter not always agreed on, to be sure, but despite these differences, the knowledge of good and evil remains a matter of the mind knowing itself through the fulfillment of all its powers. The Romantic writer closest to Alison in showing how these powers are fulfilled is William Hazlitt, who, free from the timid piety that mars Alison's criticism of tragedy, makes a full application of Alison's psychology to the problem of tragic evil.

1

Although keeping within the same empirical tradition as Alison, Hazlitt gives to creative imagination a wider sort of objectivity and a deeper penetration into truth. In "On Poetry in General" (1818) Hazlitt defines imagination as "that faculty which represents objects, not as they are in themselves, but as they are moulded by other thoughts and feelings into an infinite variety of shapes and combinations of power" (5:4).[1] All the business of life, all its "reality," is made up of perceptions shaped "according to our wishes and fancies"; but beyond the "mere delineation of natural feelings," poetry requires the "heightenings of the imagination" (5.3). In a state of intense feeling the poet's imagination ranges through established associations to find otherwise unrevealed similarities. Emotion is both a directing and a selecting principle: it guides the imagination to comparisons that will convey the poet's feeling to his audience and at the same time rejects irrelevant associations (8:42). The imaginative complex is never static. Within the limits of the controlling emotion, it is a dynamic, multiplying interaction of images, thought, and feeling. It captures the flux of actual experience, and thereby attains a kind of truth or reality inaccessible to mere reasoning or abstraction. Yet if this truth cannot be stated in propositions, neither does it exist only in the particular. It resides in the interaction of both the general and the specific. This interaction is made possible by a kind of order, established by our previous experience, which gives stability and firmness to reality both in everyday affairs and in poetry. This order comprises an infinitely numerous set of relations—founded on resemblance, contiguity, cause and effect, etc.—wherein one idea regularly recalls an associated idea or ideas. No two people share exactly the same set of associations, but Hazlitt assumes a body of common associations which a work of art must exploit in order to extend its grasp of truth.[2]

Through habitual sympathetic identification with others, the successful poet has acquired an intuitive awareness of this sort of order in human experience. In other words, Hazlitt builds the generalizing faculty of reason into the imaginative process. Reynolds gave "sound reason," conditioned by much experience, a "sagacity" which "does not wait for the slow progress of deduction" but immediately "feels and acknowledges truth."[3] Abraham Tucker went a step farther and handed habitual understanding over to the imagination. Conclusions of a sort habitually arrived at by the understanding make the imagination discriminating, so that it attains an immediate awareness of truth.[4] According to Hazlitt, whose essay "On Genius and Common Sense" (1821) was evidently influenced by both Reynolds and Tucker, repeated experience and "the law of association" furnish the mind with "a series of unpremeditated conclusions on almost all subjects that can be brought before it." Analogous to this "common sense" or "tacit reason," but differing from it in "strength and depth of feeling" and in the resulting insight, is the power of genius to select and link ideas according to firmly established associations and thus to intuit truth (8:33–36, 40–42).[5] Necessary to this intuition, of course, is habitual sympathy with others. Hazlitt criticizes many of the poets of his own time for a selfish preoccupation which limits their audience. The great poet brings to the moment of creation, when subject and object coalesce, thoughts and feelings conditioned by sympathy. Shakespeare and Milton acquired "their power over the human mind" because, free from "devouring egotism," they had gained a "deeper sense than others of what was grand in the objects of nature, or affecting in the events of human life" (5:53).[6] A work of art achieves general truth, not by abstracting to any kind of central form, but through presenting objects seen and therefore molded by an artist whose wide and sympathetic experience has made him immediately feel their universal force. The success of a poem assumes a similar (although never of course identical) and responsive set of associations in the reader, which enables him to create his own version of truth.

117

2

For Hazlitt, the ultimate test of art is the sort of truth just described. This fusion of generally affecting images is beautiful as well as true. The sublime, as Hazlitt occasionally defines it, is the highest kind of beauty: it is the most intense kind, and in its intensity it aggregates widely ranging trains of ideas which bring all the resources of the mind to the moment of creation.

Of course, like others, Hazlitt also uses the word *sublime* in many conventional and not very precise ways. These are related more or less clearly to power or magnitude of some sort. Hazlitt finds sublimity in Satan in *Paradise Lost* ("the most heroic subject that ever was chosen for a poem") (5:63, 66; 6:317); in Lear's "gigantic, outspread sorrows" (18:332; cf. 6:348; 16:61; 18:334) and in his appeal to, and identification with, the heavens (18:335; 16:63); in the "mental fortitude and heroic cast of thought" in tragic characters (6:355); in "eastern magnificence" (5:197); in the "intensity" of Kemble's acting (5:379); in Faustus's desire for unbounded knowledge (6:202–203); in Sir Thomas Browne's abstruse researches, which lose "the finite" in "the infinite" (6:333); in Coriolanus's "imaginary superiority" to others (18:290); in Hector's death (4:224); in "Martin's sceptical indifference to moral good and evil" in *Candide* (5:114); in the "colloquy of man's nature with itself" in *The Duchess of Malfi* (6:246); in the "sweetness and majesty" of Christ's "humanity" (6:183); and in "the pyramids of Egypt, . . . a Gothic ruin, or an old Roman encampment" (5:52). In a passage recalling the frequent distinction between the sublime and the pathetic, Hazlitt says that the pyramids, the ruin, and the encampment affect us "with admiration and delight" in the manner of epic poetry, whereas dramatic poetry "affects us by sympathy," filling us "with terror and pity" (5:52). Hazlitt does not, of course, ordinarily restrict the sublime to the epic or to descriptive passages, nor does he make sublimity depend on physical size, its accoutrements, or its peculiar lineaments. In tragedy Hazlitt's sublime is the sublime of vision. In that tragedy which Hazlitt cites as sublime more often than any other work, Lear's speech " 'The little dogs and all, Tray, Blanche, and Sweetheart, see they bark at me!' " depends not at all on anything "romantic, quaint, mysterious in the objects introduced. . . . The whole sublimity of the passage is from the weight of passion thrown into it, and this is the poet's own doing" (12:341; cf. 6:363).

Hazlitt provides a measure for this "weight of passion" in his distinction between the sublime and the beautiful. Usually *beauty* is Hazlitt's more general term, describing everything that gives aesthetic pleasure. Sometimes, as in two of the examples in the preceding paragraph (5:63 and 6:317), Hazlitt seems to pair the words *sublime* and *beautiful* to emphasize intensity or simply artistic success rather than to designate a combination of different qualities. On the other hand, even when he does distinguish between beauty and sublimity, he sees no reason why they cannot exist together in the same work of art. Hazlitt distinguishes between sublimity and beauty most clearly in "On the Elgin Marbles" (1822). Here he uses the word *grandeur* more frequently than *sublimity*, but apparently the two words mean the same thing, the former being applied especially to painting and the latter more generally to poetry. "On the Elgin Marbles" takes issue with Sir Joshua Reynolds's thesis that "the pure standard of truth and beauty" requires abstracting to "a *middle central form* . . . by leaving out the pecularities of all the others" (18:164).[7] In an earlier essay, "On the Ideal" (1815), Hazlitt explains that, in order to find an ideal form to "express" any quality, the artist must *select* the right model rather than abstract from many models. The model must then be painted with all the emotion-charged specific details expressing the quality which the artist wishes to represent and for which the model was selected. The particulars that initiate the trains of ideas must be those which the artist has perceived and modified in a state of intense feeling and not features which have been emotionally discharged by an intervening process of abstraction. These latter would "leave nothing for his imagination, or the imagination of the spectator to work upon" (18:78–79; see also 4:68; 20:388–90).

Both grandeur and beauty require details of this sort. The former *"aggrandises,"* the latter *"harmonises . . .* our impressions of things" (18:164). Grandeur combines its particulars in "masses" that with their "extraordinary strength, magnitude, &c. or in a word, . . . [their] excess of power . . . startle and overawe the mind" (18:163, 164–65). If grandeur is "the principle of connexion between different parts," then "beauty is the principle of affinity between different forms, or their gradual conversion into each other" (18:164). The superficial similarity to Burke is evident. Beauty "blends and harmonises different powers or qualities together, so as to produce a soft and pleasurable sensation" (18:165).[8] In each case details may be precisely rendered but, of course, they must be subordinated to the general effect. Obviously the two effects—of "massing" and "blending," respectively—may exist together, although one may be more pronounced than the other. Hazlitt does not find any "incompatibility between strength and softness," sublimity and beauty. Nature includes both extremes, and both qualities distinguish the greatest art, although an artist, like Guido, may be "more soft than strong," or, like Rembrandt, "more strong than soft" (18:166).

Hazlitt's insistence on particulars is not at the expense of the sublime. Like Alison, he considers the unity of "emotion" or of "character" or "expression" to be the essential aim, and, again like Alison, he does not believe that the unity is violated by particulars as long as they contribute to the expression. In painting, Hazlitt finds the "general effect" of grandeur not only in the representation of physical mass but also in "a certain character stamped upon the different features," as in a Titian portrait (18:163). Here Hazlitt is very close to Alison. Grandeur does not require qualities connected with size, physical or moral, but, rather, a "unity of intention" toward which "a number of particulars" are combined (18: 163). In poetry visible mass is even less important to sublimity than it is in painting. What counts is the "weight of passion," as we have seen in the illustration from *King Lear,* and "unity of impression," "the slightest want" of which "destroys the sublime" (6:23–24). The two go together, for intensity of passion not only stimulates the linking of associated ideas but excludes irrelevancies. Therefore, when Hazlitt says that *"grandeur consists in connecting a number of parts into a whole, and not leaving out the parts"* (18:162), he is not making out a case for exact copying; he means, rather, "not leaving out any parts, *no matter how small* (such as 'the little dogs'), *that will intensify the 'unity of impression.'* " In this sort of sublimity the idea of size persists, but it is psychological size, not visible size. This conception of mass is evident in the "weight" of mind-filling passion and in the "aggregating" of a large number of images—a kind of sublime size suggested by Johnson's concern for integrating images into metaphor,[9] implied in Alison's equation of additional trains with increased pleasure, and made explicit by Hazlitt in his essay "On Wit and Humour" (1819). It is by "finding out something similar in things generally alike, or with like feelings attached to them" that the imagination brings "the general forms and aggregate masses of our ideas . . . more into play, to give weight and magnitude" (6:23). Johnson, too, had said that "sublimity is produced by aggregation," and the similarity of the contexts as well as the phrasing suggests that Hazlitt had Johnson's *Life of Cowley* in mind, for in affirming the cognitive power of metaphor both Johnson and Hazlitt contrast the aggregation of sublimity with the dispersion of wit. Wit, says Hazlitt, makes use of "merely accidental and nominal resemblances" in order "to disconnect our sympathy from passion and power, [rather] than . . . to confirm, enforce, and expand them by powerful and lasting associations of ideas, or striking and true analogies" (6.23).

The creative imagination attains sublime extension and power by fusing even widely disparate materials. Hazlitt's view of tragic unity allows a much greater diversity of material—and consequent diversity of tone—than Alison's. Shakespeare takes the widest possible range, but from that very range he has his choice of the greatest variety and aptitude of materials. He brings together images the most alike, but placed at the greatest distance from each other; that is, found in circumstances of the greatest dissimilitude. From the remoteness of his combinations, and the celerity with which they are effected, they coalesce the more indissolubly together. The more the thoughts are strangers to each other, and the longer they have been kept asunder, the more intimate does their union seem to become. Their felicity is equal to their force. Their likeness is made more dazzling by their novelty. They startle, and take the fancy prisoner in the same instant (5.53–54).

The "distance" of the images from each other is not measurable in miles or minutes but in "dissimilitude" of associations. Yet the emotion is so intense that—drawn together by other, similar associations—the images are fused the more solidly for their momentary disparateness. In *King Lear* Hazlitt finds "the sublimest instance [he knows] of passion and wit united." Lear and the Fool represent extremes in association which are both pulled together and kept apart as the latter counterpoints "on a meaner scale" Lear's catalog of follies, until the moment when Lear, with his pity for the "poor naked wretches," identifies himself with the Fool and other unfortunates. This moment of aggregation is "sublime" (6:24; see also 4:26).

3

In placing the sublime within the frame of the beautiful and in identifying the sublime principally with the tragic, Hazlitt stands apart from Coleridge, Wordsworth, and De Quincey, and in making tragedy the "most impassioned species" of poetry and therefore the most sublime (5:5), he differs from Blake, Shelley, and Hunt, as well. To explain why tragedy pleases, Hazlitt draws on a number of the usual reasons. He scorns the "professed moralist in literature" and the crude poetic justice in plays like *The London Merchant* (16:6),[10] but he draws on the affective hypothesis to find that tragedy curbs dangerous emotions and encourages benevolent ones. Tragedy "corrects [the] fatal excesses [of the passions] in ourselves by pointing to the greater extent of sufferings and of crimes to which they have led others." On the other hand, through pity, tragedy "makes man a partaker with his kind" (4:200; see also 4:306). What we are purged of is not pity and fear but selfishness. "In proportion to the greatness of the evil, is our sense and desire of the opposite good excited; and . . . our sympathy with actual suffering is lost in the strong impulses given to our natural affections, and carried away with the swelling tide of passion, that gushes from and relieves the heart" (4:272; see also 5:5).[11] Here, in these sympathetic pleasures, Hazlitt is close to Burke, as he is again when he points to "the common love of strong excitement" as a further reason why tragedy pleases. He agrees with Burke that an audience would empty the theater where they had been watching a tragedy, in order to see "a public execution in the next street" (5:7).[12] But there is an important difference from Burke. When Hazlitt writes that "the pleasure . . . derived from tragic poetry, is not any thing peculiar to it as poetry, as a fictitious and fanciful thing" (5:7), the last six words are crucial. Hazlitt does not mean that tragedy offers *only* the kind of pleasure available at a public hanging but that *insofar as strong excitement is enjoyable,* a tragedy and a hanging have exactly the same kind of appeal. As something with its own kind of reality, however, tragedy offers the additional pleasure of *knowing* evil. Hazlitt has extended Burke's sublime agitation to stimulate the whole process of thought.

Strong excitement in itself is not enough. We have the power to *feel,* and we enjoy the exercise of that power regardless of the kind of feeling. "It is as natural to hate as to love, to despise as to admire, to express our hatred or contempt, as our love or admiration" (5:7). But we also enjoy the power of knowing the thing we hate, and Shakespeare's tragedies, says Hazlitt, give us this power by defining the objects of our feeling precisely. This definition, obviously, cannot exist in a series of propositions dissecting evil or enumerating its forms, causes, and effects. If we share the values and certain basic experiences of the audience for which Shakespeare wrote *Lear,* we could readily compile such a list without reading or seeing the play. What we could not do, unless we knew the play, is to accept, reject, or modify its pattern of pain and death as part of the reality within ourselves. Poetry sees nature "through the medium of passion and imagination, not divested of that medium by means of literal truth or abstract reason" (5:8). We know evil, as we know any kind of reality, by the creative act in which the evil person or action merges into the complex of sensation, thought, and feeling that our sensory, intellectual, and emotional experience is continually validating. "Impassioned poetry" appeals to all our faculties. It is "an emanation of the moral and intellectual part of our nature, as well as of the sensitive." Because the "domestic or prose" tragedies of George Lillo and Edward Moore appeal almost exclusively to "our sensibility," they "oppress and lie like a dead weight upon the mind, a load of misery which it is unable to throw off." On the other hand "the tragedy of Shakspeare . . . stirs our inmost affections; abstracts evil from itself by combining it with all the forms of imagination, and with the deepest workings of the heart, and rouses the whole man within us" (5:6). There is no question but that the audience finds sublimity pathetic and agitating. In Shakespeare's tragedies, " 'while rage with rage does sympathise' " (5:52), the passion calls "into play all the resources of the understanding and all the energies of the will" (5:51). Although tragedy arrives at its knowledge of evil in a way different from that offered by a moral fable, it continues to give the will a moral impetus and direction. At the same time as we come to loathe the evil, we like "to indulge our hatred and scorn of it; . . . to grapple with it in thought, in action, to sharpen our intellect, to arm our will against it, to know the worst we have to contend with, and to contend with it to the utmost" (5:7).

But Hazlitt's delight in knowing evil is more than a matter of readying ourselves for moral action. It comes closer than that to Knight's pleasure in sharing energetic emotions. Hazlitt is a long way from Alison's appreciation of evil characters only for their illumination of virtue in other characters. We enjoy seeing evil displayed "in all the splendour of deformity" (5:7). Shakespeare's villains have admirably energetic qualities. Iago is detestable but intellectually acute (4:206). Regarding Iago's attractive vigor, Hazlitt follows Knight in distinguishing between an evil character's malignancy and his admirable energies. Iago's role would "hardly be tolerated, even as a foil to the virtue and generosity of the other characters in the play, but for its indefatigable industry and inexhaustible resources, which divert the attention of the spectator (as well as his own) from the end he has in view to the means by which it must be accomplished" (4:209). For Edmund, another "light-hearted" villain, we can make a similar distinction (4:209, 259). In Richard III Hazlitt finds the same "mixture of intellectual vigour with moral depravity" and regrets that, in the production he is reviewing, cuts and revisions have only made "Richard as odious and disgusting as possible" (4:300). Both Knight and Hazlitt respect energy. A passive life of satisfied desire is incomplete. It is as the human soul rages against destruction, says Hazlitt, that it completes itself in the full play of its resources (4:258; 5:51–52). But the energy of passion that, according to Knight, the audience shares with tragic characters is in itself not enough for Hazlitt. Hazlitt, like Blake, believes that the redeeming energy of great art brings the whole mind into harmonious action. The audience witnessing a great tragedy may enjoy Iago's, Edmund's, or Richard's remarkable vigor, but unlike these characters and unlike Knight it cannot split its response off from the "moral and intellectual part of our nature."

The knowledge that "the whole man within us" arrives at has little to do with theology or other speculative systems. Of course Hazlitt is talking not about evil that can be overcome by technology, legislation, education, or any sort of indoctrination but about more deeply seated evil—pain and death and the self-regarding excesses that visit pain and death on others. No system of belief kept Hazlitt from recognizing life as essentially tragic. For all his life-long defense of the

French Revolution and his active support of radical causes, he did not believe that any political action could insure men's happiness. He was far from believing in Godwinian perfectibility or in the utilitarian's more modest faith in progress.[13] He suspected any sort of philosophical system, for, if fully accepted, any such system will check the probing of association, the aggregation of ideas, and the mind's use of all its resources.[14]

Regarding Greek religion and its inhibiting of the imagination, Hazlitt echoes Coleridge.[15] In Greek "religion, or mythology," the description of a higher power is "material and definite," whereas in the Christian religion "we find only unlimited, undefined power . . . [and] belief of an universal, invisible Principle of all things, a vastness and obscurity which confounds our perceptions, while it exalts our piety" (16:65–66). Hazlitt, of course, is not objecting to visible firmness in art but to solidifying the powers of both god and nature in anthropomorphic forms. Greek sculpture is a work of the imagination, but, according to Hazlitt in this passage, it leaves no place for the imagination to go. Greek poetry is similarly restrictive in subjecting the imagination to the senses rather than in allowing the senses to serve the imagination. Less anthropomorphic in its myths, Christianity allows greater freedom in linking up trains of ideas. When it comes to tragedy, Hazlitt has more concern for imaginative scope than for "exalting our piety." His "Christian mythology," like the Protestant dissent characterizing his political essays, defines an attitude rather than a doctrine. Authority —in religion, politics, or art—should not stand between any man and the truth.

Hazlitt's practical criticism of tragedy—which appears principally in his *Characters of Shakespear's Plays* (1817) and *A View of the English Stage* (1818)—can hardly be understood to mean that an enlightened audience recognizes in tragic misfortunes the workings of any "universal, invisible Principle of all things." Hazlitt's definition of tragedy is based on Shakespeare. In Shakespeare, Hazlitt encountered a tragic world put into order not by extrahuman controls but by the artist's design and the characters' thought and action. Shakespeare's ethical values are firmly Christian, but his tragedies do not demonstrate the Christian pattern of death and salvation or, for that matter, any providential concern for man's choice of right or wrong. Set speeches, like Ulysses' in *Troilus and Cressida*, may caution against offending universal order, but the action of this play, like the action of the great tragedies, offers little support for this warning.[16] Shakespeare's tragedies tell us a great deal about good and evil—and to that extent about the nature of the universe—but their growing moral penetration shows itself in the self-knowing identity that guilt and suffering bring to the principal characters and not in the allocation of rewards and punishments.[17]

In Shakespeare's tragedies, Hazlitt realizes, disaster enriches character and character grows into a more comprehensive role than it had in Greek tragedy, where the moral issues are defined and resolved by action. Geoffrey Brereton has pointed out that in Shakespeare "it is no longer realistic to separate [Aristotle's] 'thought' from either 'action' or 'character,' even for the purpose of analysis. One . . . must recognize that 'thought' is at once an internal action inseparable from the external action and a factor in the composition of 'character' " (pp. 95–96). Character that includes thought as action brings order out of the moral confusion, precluding the need for a neatly fitted sequence of events. Greek tragedy, says Hazlitt, depends for its "beauty and grandeur" on the close "imitation" of "the external object," i.e., the imitation of an action. "Hence the Unities: for, in order to identify the imitation as much as possible with the reality, and leave nothing to mere imagination, it was necessary to give the same coherence and consistency to the different parts of a story, as to the different limbs of a statue." English tragedy, on the other hand, attains grandeur through a less circumscribed—and hence more sublime—kind of aggregation, for it "seeks to identify the original impression with whatever else, within the range of thought or feeling, can strengthen, relieve, adorn or elevate it" (6:350). Sublime integrity does not require the imitation of one action limited in time and place; it may be none the less firm, as well as truer and more beautiful, in the "powerful and lasting association of ideas or striking and true analogies" (6:23). "Shakespear's mastery over his subject . . . was owing to a knowledge of the connecting links of the passions, and their effect upon the mind, still more wonderful than any systematic adherence to rules" (4:260).[18]

We would be wrong, therefore, to look in Shakespeare's tragedies for a kind of order ascribable either to philosophical systems or to critical rigidities which, says Hazlitt, were derived from theological ones. Nevertheless, Hazlitt finds order in these plays, but it is an order inherent in the work itself and not in anything external to it. It may be in the integrity of the poet's design, in the wholeness of individual character, in the character's reordering of his broken world, or in all of these. Hazlitt's examination of tragedy and tragic characters suggests in a general way the two stages of sublime experience described by Kant: temporary bafflement—a "confounding of our perceptions"—followed by an expansion of the mind as it comprehends a higher order of magnitude.[19] Rather than Kant's "reason," however, it is feeling carried "to the utmost point of sublimity or pathos"—it is the "imaginary exaggeration" of suffering, the "unlimited indulgence" of pity or terror—that "brings every moment of our being or object of nature in startling review before us; and in the rapid whirl of events, lifts us from the depths of woe to the highest contemplations on human life" (5:5). This expansion of the mind is a continuous process of coalescence running through individual metaphors, extended passages, and ultimately the whole work (5:5; 5:54; 6:24). The chaos with which Shakespeare's tragic world confronts the audience falls into order as the mind enlarges to comprehend the whole. The characters in *Othello* and "the images they stamp upon the mind are the farthest asunder possible, the distance between them is immense: yet the compass of knowledge and invention which the poet has shown in embodying these extreme creations of his genius is only greater than the truth and felicity with which he has identified each character with itself, or blended their different qualities together in the same story" (4:200–201). "The whole play [of *Macbeth*] is an unruly chaos of strange and forbidden things, where the ground rocks under our feet," yet "the absolute truth and identity" of Macbeth's character is never lost "in the fluctuations of fortune or the storm of passion" (4:191-92). Shakespeare keeps up "the distinction . . . in nature, between the understandings and the moral habits of men" (4:237), yet he reconciles these differences in integrity of character and, for his tragic heroes, in the unfolding of their thought. In *Lear* the "tug and war of the elements of our being . . . and the giddy anarchy and whirling tumult of the thoughts" (4:258) are ordered by the mind of Lear. Lear begins the play with a comfortable selection of values which he regards as absolute. Disaster exposes their inadequacy. In a passage underlined in Keats's copy of the *Characters of Shakespear's Plays*, Hazlitt approvingly quotes Charles Lamb:

> The greatness of Lear is not in corporal dimension, but in intellectual; the explosions of his passion are terrible as a volcano: they are storms turning up and disclosing to the bottom that rich sea, his mind, with all its vast riches. . . . In the aberrations of his reason, we discover a mighty irregular power of reasoning, immethodised from the ordinary purposes of life, but exerting its powers, as the wind blows where it listeth, at will on the corruptions and abuses of mankind. (4:271)[20]

To this ordering process the tragic actor must bring resources of his own. Mrs. Siddons's action was "the perfection of tragedy" because it combined "passion . . . with lofty imagination and commanding intellect" to confront "scenes of terror and agony" with "the full plenitude and expansion of her being" and so, in this self-organizing fulfillment, to rise "superior to nature and fortune" (18:196).[21] If Hazlitt prefers, for tragedy, what he calls the Christian mythology over the Greek mythology, it is not because the former discloses more acceptable dogma but because it allows the imagination (the poet's, the character's, the reader's) freedom to range far and wide and to coalesce its disparate materials into its own kind of order.

In the eighteenth century, we have seen, a feeling of infinite size and power was often credited to the sublime. If the sublime described by Hazlitt suggests the infinite, it obviously does so in a different way from the natural sublime of Addison, Baillie, Burke, and Gerard. The measure of natural sublimity—and the emotional gauge of all sublime objects—is visual extension, especially beyond actually visible limits. One might find an analogy in the boundless interaction of the sensations, feelings, and thoughts that build up Hazlitt's "sublime aggregation." But this multiplicity is not responsible for sublime feelings in the same manner as the infinite extension posited by Addison and others. Large objects, according to Addison and his followers, extend the mind along the coordinates of space and time toward an idea of God's infinite magnitude or at least to a feeling of accomplishment like that which follows some difficult physical act. The expansion described by Hazlitt, on the other hand, cannot be plotted on these coordinates. This expansion comprehends widely ranging materials, but it is not an operation that has much in common with exploring space. Its dimensions are exclusively mental. They are qualitative, not quantitative. The aggregating of diverse materials into Hazlitt's sublime repudiates abstractions such as space and time, for the imagination creates truth in the continuous fusion of the particular and the general. If the mind comes to rest on an abstraction cut off from any sensory impact and its emotional force, the process stops and the mind settles for an inferior kind of truth.

Despite its fluidity, this truth is neither indefinite nor formless nor merely subjective. The images "coalesce indissolubly," for instance, in a tragic character's "identity" and in the unity of a play or any work of art. To be sure, this identity and this unity may not be—probably cannot be—exactly the same for any two people or even for the same person at two different times. Yet when the poet has been conditioned through habitual sympathetic identification to recognize what is important to many people, his imagination stimulates the reader or audience to engage in a creative act structured after his own. When the emotion is so intense that association brings all the faculties into harmonious action, the created reality comprises the keenest insight, the securest values, and an impetus to action. Tragedy, since it is the "most impassioned species" of poetry, brings this process to its consummation.

CHAPTER NINE

KEATS

Keats, like Hazlitt, applies the word *sublime* to a creative act of the imagination in a state of intense excitement. If this kind of sublimity is determined by magnitude, it is magnitude encompassing mental activity rather than physical extension. This mental activity creates a kind of truth that, in its superiority to time and space, can get the better of pain and suffering. Keats's ideas of the imagination and its disposition of tragic disagreeables owe more than a little to Hazlitt, and it will be useful to look into these resemblances; but Keats goes beyond Hazlitt in refining the sublime of vision and in specifying its power over the tragic disagreeables.[1] Since Keats was a poet with a growing interest in tragedy, we are fortunate in being able to examine his practice as well as his theory.

1

Keats's best known statement on the disagreeables, written in his "Negative Capability" letter of December 1817, describes Benjamin West's painting *Death on the Pale Horse*:

It is a wonderful picture, when West's age is considered; But there is nothing to be intense upon; no women one feels mad to kiss; no face swelling into reality. the excellence of every Art is its intensity, capable of making all disagreeables evaporate, from their being in close relationship with Beauty & Truth—Examine King Lear & you will find this examplified throughout; but in this picture we have unpleasantness without any momentous depth of speculation excited, in which to bury its repulsiveness— (1:192)[2]

This statement raises three immediate questions: (1) What does Keats mean by the "disagreeables"? (2) How does intensity "evaporate" the disagreeables by putting them "in close relationship with Beauty & Truth"? and (3) "How does a "momentous depth of speculation . . . bury . . . repulsiveness"?

Keats is not using the word *disagreeables* as Addison used it when, speaking of a garden recreated in the imagination, he said that well-traveled "Pleasure Traces" in the mind quickly stop up any traces that belonged to "disagreeable Ideas" (*Spectator* 417). Addison meant that the imagination, dominated by the pleasure-giving objects in the garden, soon omits any memory of unpleasant objects or details such as, presumably, withered trees, misshapen rocks, and ugly bare spots. It had long been recognized, at least as early as Hobbes, that intense emotion channels ideas in trains associated with the dominant feeling and suppresses those associations not congruent with this feeling.[3] But Keats does not mean that the imagination must exclude the unpleasant objects. In his picture of *Death on the Pale Horse*, West's imagination could not have excluded death, any more than a tragedy could exclude pain and suffering. What West should have evaporated, according to Keats, but didn't, was the *disagreeableness* of death—not by prettying it up, but by representing it truly.

Like other Romantic poets or critics, Keats finds truth not in the deductions of logic but in the imaginative fusion of sensory particulars with thought and feeling (1:185; 2: 213).[4] Keats's preference "for a Life of Sensations rather than of Thoughts" (1:185) does not, of course, exclude thought from this imaginative coalescence but emphasizes the primary importance of conveying both thought and feeling through concrete particulars. To create the truth that is also beauty, the poet must select and shape sensory particulars to suggest the "essence" or "character" of an object or experience. This essence is not an abstract idea existing apart from any perception of it, but, rather, it is a perception in which thought and feeling mold details to display the ordering power of the poet's mind. The resulting creation attains a kind of permanence beyond the evanescence of sensory phenomena. This permanence may exist in the importance of the creative moment to the poet himself—a moment to which the realization of imaginative power gives a value not measurable by any clock. Or permanence may further exist in a reflection of general human experience. Beyond the "reality" or "truth" which the poet finds for himself in any imaginative perception, lies the network of innumerable associations uniting mankind's thought and feeling with the sensory world. For communication, the poet must always choose particulars with associations shared by his readers, but poetry attains what Keats considered a higher reality if the poet shares the widespread associations linking man with nature and his fellow men.[5] This sharing calls for a certain loss of identity; through identification with others, a poet must come to know what is moving and important in their lives. This knowledge adds another dimension of permanence to his comprehension of essence.

Necessary to any sort of poetic truth or reality—whether or not of the highest sort—is "fellowship with essence . . . / Full alchemiz'd, and free of space . . ." (*Endymion*, bk. 1, ll. 779–80). To liberate the ordered permanence of essence from the chaos of sensation, the imagination must be empowered by the emotion Keats sometimes describes as "sublime." "All of our Passions," Keats wrote a month before his criticism of West, "are . . . in their sublime, creative of essential Beauty" (1:184). "Essential Beauty" is a tautology—all beauty, for

Keats, captures essence. In this passage "sublime" implies intensity.

Keats does not use the word *sublime* (or its various forms) very frequently or consistently. In eleven of twenty-one appearances, the word implies only some sort of elevation —in emotion, style, mass, or power (four times, in the poems, it refers to preternatural beings).[6] In the remaining appearances, the word suggests—in varying degrees of specificity—a process of separating out some desirable quality or product from grosser materials. Glaucus, with a "backward glance sublime," would breathe away the "slime" so that his true nature might emerge (*Endymion*, bk. 3, ll. 329–32). While Keats had neglected to answer a letter from Bailey, his "nature" had lain "dormant" until, having received still another letter from Bailey, he was "self spiritualized" from this neglectful self-indulgence "into a kind of sublime Misery" (1:173). Likewise, Wordsworth's "more remote and sublimer muse" (2:94) escapes the self-indulgence of his "egotistical sublime" (1:387). America's great men, Keats believes, "can never reach the sublime," for they cannot rise above their material interests (1:397–98). In "something of material sublime" in "The Epistle to Reynolds," Stuart M. Sperry finds Keats ironically juxtaposing the imagination's demands for both the essential and the concrete (1:261).[7] Sublime passion separates essence not from sensation but from the impermanence of a world known only through the senses and from the disagreeableness of such impermanence. The poetic imagination always requires sensory particulars with associations that suggest the permanent. On one occasion Keats describes the flow of wide-ranging association as, under the impetus and direction of emotion, it links sensory details with essential truth: in the "Sublimity" that welcomes him home, his imagination adds "particles" to his "mighty abstract Idea . . . of Beauty" and so expands his mind until it merges with the infinite (1:403–404). Once more, sublime magnitude becomes unmeasurable by physical extension. Keats was more interested in visionary reality. In his description of Ambleside falls (although here he does not use the word *sublime*), he distinguishes, in their expansive effects, between physical magnitude and "the intellect, the countenance of such places." It is the character of the falls rather than their sheer size that surpasses his imagination and makes Keats forget his stature.[8] He will "learn poetry here and . . . henceforth write more than ever, for the abstract endeavor of being able to add a mite to that mass of beauty which is harvested from these grand materials, by the finest spirits, and put into etherial existence for the relish of one's fellows" (1:301).

The words *essence, abstraction, sublime,* and *evaporation* —like the closely related term *ethereal*—are part of a cluster of scientific terms which, Sperry has pointed out, refer to distillation and therefore suggest an analogy to the creative process (pp. 37–49).[9] Distillation is a process using heat to drive off vapor from liquids or solids and then condensing this vapor into what were sometimes called "spirits" or "essences." These were valued for unusual properties or powers. They were said to have been *abstracted* from the undesirable residue. *Sublimation* means "dry distillation"—that is, a process wherein a heated substance passes from the solid to the gaseous state and again condenses to a solid without liquefying. *Evaporation* could refer to a kind of distillation in which the unessential portion of a substance is driven off while the valued part remains behind. Even though *sublimation* and *evaporation* refer to processes of distillation that are really opposite of each other, these meanings sharpen Keats's use of the terms to separate essences from disagreeables. Through its apparent association with his scientific studies, *ethereal* is another term that sheds some light on Keats's idea of the imagination. Ether, a substance believed to permeate interplanetary and stellar space and to fill the interstices between particles of air and other matter on earth, was regarded as the medium through which light and heat are transmitted. Unlike solids, fluids, and gases, it could not be confined and could be known only through its action on other matter. Equated by Keats to the "unearthly" and "spiritual" (1:395), the *ethereal* sounds very much like essence. But a difference can sometimes be detected. Both words describe truth purged of disagreeables in order to become beautiful, but whereas *essence* emphasizes the purity of the product, *ethereal* stresses the release from worldly encumbrances. As the medium for transmitting heat, ether would be necessary to distillation, which requires heat just as the imagination requires intensity to effect its transmutations. But an analogy at least equally illuminating is to the product rather than the process of the imagination. This product may be accurately called, as Keats calls it in *Endymion*, "unconfin'd" (bk. 3, l. 25), for—like ether—it has been released from the causal rigidities of time and space as the imagination stretches toward the eternal. It is also unconfined (although Keats probably did not intend this suggestion) even by the poet's own mind, for among his readers it is susceptible to further transformations.

Keats's meaning of *truth* in his criticism of West's *Death on the Pale Horse* is brought into clearer focus by Hazlitt's article on the same painting in *The Edinburgh Magazine* for December 1817 (18:135–40). Keats probably had read this article. The "Descriptive Catalogue" of the exhibition, Hazlitt reports, describes *Death on the Pale Horse* as exciting the "general effect" of "the *Terrible Sublime.*" Hazlitt objects that the picture lacks "imagination" and "gusto." "Gusto in art," Hazlitt explains elsewhere, "is power or passion defining any object" or, in other words, it is emotion delineating that "precise association with pleasure or pain" which constitutes the object's "character" (4:77). It is that intensity of feeling which, by stimulating the imagination to select and organize particulars with generally moving associations, expresses the "truth of character" (i.e., the "internal character" or "living principle") of an object. Lacking gusto, West's painting does not get to the center of things. It "gives merely the rim and outline . . . in a vivid and dazzling, but confused and imperfect manner" (18:136). It fails to "represent the force of moral truth" in the only way a painter can do this: "by substituting heiroglyphics for words, and presenting the closest and most striking affinities his fancy and observation can suggest between the general idea and the visible illustration of it" (18:136–38). West's Death is not true to general feelings about death.

> He has not the calm, still, majestic form of Death, killing by a look,—withering by a touch. His presence does not make the still air cold. His flesh is not stony or cadaverous, but is crusted over with a yellow glutinous paste, as if it had been baked in a pye. Milton makes Death "grin horrible a ghastly smile," with an evident allusion to the common Death's head; but in the picture he seems grinning for a wager, with a full row of loose rotten teeth. . . . We have no idea of such a swaggering and blustering Death as this of Mr. West's. He has not invoked a ghastly spectre from the tomb, but has called up an old squalid ruffian from a night cellar, and crowned him "monarch of the universal world." (18:138)

That is, West has not presented death truly—not with the calm majesty and withering touch that we associate with death, nor with the *"common* Death's Head" suggested by Milton (who like Shakespeare sensed what is "affecting in the events of human life" [5:53]).[10] We find West's "squalid ruffian" unpleasant, not because he represents death but because he is outside our experience and associations with death. West's "visible illustration," therefore, fails to carry the "character" of death home to the imagination. "The moral impression of Death is essentially visionary; its reality is in the mind's eye" (18:137). It is not the picture's subject but the picture's *untruth* that Hazlitt finds disagreeable, just as he found the tragedies of Lillo and Edward Moore, because of the lack of truth, oppressive and lying "like a dead weight upon the mind" (5:6). The painting is terrible without being sublime because its truth has not escaped from the narrowness of idiosyncrasy into moral "reality."

Keats, it would seem, makes the same objection to West's painting—that is, the disagreeableness of painful subjects like death is not evaporated unless the artist, through his intensity of feeling, represents the essential quality (the beautiful truth) of his subject. Keats does not become explicit, as Hazlitt does, on the need for general associations to serve the truth. But there is no doubt that he, too, makes the expression of truth depend on shared associations. The need for a common ground of association is implicit in Keats's account of "negative capability," with which, in the same letter, Keats follows the comment on West. In his contentment with "half knowledge," the negatively capable artist or poet surrenders his preconceptions and his presumption to knowing the whole truth (1:193–94). Without this modesty, the poet will deceive himself with statements unsupported by his own imagination and unsupportable by his reader's. As Keats said later, poetry must not try to "bully" us "into a certain Philosophy" (1:223–24); instead it must "strike the Reader as a wording of his own highest thoughts, and appear almost a Remembrance" (1:238). If the reader, stimulated by concrete particulars, is to draw on his own resources of thought and feeling in an act of creation, he must share with the poet a network of association. Keats comments on the diversity of points— tipping "the fine Webb of [the] Soul"—from which a man may "weave a tapestry empyrean"; yet, although "Minds . . . traverse each other in Numberless points, . . . all [at] last greet each other at the Journeys end." A man and his neighbor may reach the ethereal together if, in recounting his journey, the man does not "dispute or assert" but only "whispers" his results (1:231–32). Also enriching a tapestry of association is that other form of unselfing that Keats called the "poetical Character," which has "no identity" of its own but is "continually . . . filling some other Body" (1:386–87).[11] It is this loss of self which, in Hazlitt's words, enabled Shakespeare to know what is "affecting in the events of human life." Only when the poet possesses both negative capability and the poetical character will his intense feeling separate the permanence of the essential from the transient residue of the personal.

Keats knew—as Sperry says very well—that in its efforts "to expel all 'disagreeables' . . . the work of art can fatally remove itself from that wealth of human knowledge and experience that provides the substratum of all aesthetic apprehension" (p. 125). In fact, on the basis of its contact with this substratum, Keats ranks the various kinds of reality that aesthetic experience can attain. On 13 March 1818 he wrote:

> Ethereal thing[s] may at least be thus real, divided under three heads—Things real—things semireal—and no things—Things real—such as existences of Sun Moon & Stars and passages of Shakspeare—Things semireal such as Love, the Clouds &c which require a greeting of the Spirit to make them wholly exist—and Nothings which are made Great and dignified by an ardent pursuit—Which by the by stamps the burgundy mark on the bottles of our Minds, insomuch as they are able to *"consec[r]ate whate'er they look upon."* (1:242–43)[12]

All three kinds of "ethereal things"—"Things real—things semireal—and no things"—must be regarded as products of the imagination created by the fusion of sensory detail with thought and feeling. At the top of the scale are the "Sun Moon & Stars" equated, in their reality, with "passages of Shakspeare." Keats found Shakespeare preeminent not only in negative capability (1:193) but also in poetical character with no identity of its own (1:387). Thus Shakespeare's imagination, unchecked by presumptions of full knowledge or by a stubborn identity, ranged freely to select those association-charged particulars "most affecting . . . in human life" and therefore, in the fusion of these particulars with thought and feeling, attained the objectivity that Keats implies by "Things real"—i.e., things as stable a part of human life as the "Sun Moon & Stars." Evidently the "Love" which shares the semireality of "Clouds" is less stable. Like Shakespeare's poetry, love is a creation of the imagination, but here it represents a narrower range of identification with others even though the lover may identify himself with the loved one or with other lovers. This semireal love, however, is still unselfing enough (see *Endymion*, bk. 1, ll. 777ff.) to bring the lover closer to the "real" than "Nothings" will do. "Nothings," although made "Great" by intensity, do not extend the imagination as far into the network of common associations as either love or passages of Shakespeare. They are even less stable than the clouds. An example of "Nothings" would probably be the "mere sophistication" of "O thou whose face hath felt the Winter's wind," which may only "neighbour to any truths" (1:233). In this poem a number of concrete objects are molded by the imagination, but the poem's "truth" lies in its fidelity to Keats's feeling of the moment and not in wide-ranging links with human experience.

The passage has been otherwise interpreted. For their fulfillment, says Bate, the "real," the "semireal," and "Nothings" require successively a greater contribution from the human mind or heart. "Some things, certainly 'real,' may not require this 'greeting of the Spirit.' But others—at least 'things semireal'—do require that greeting, that contribution, for their fulfillment; and this union of the perceiving mind and the perceived object should not be confused with mere 'Nothings' that are solely the product of human desires" (p. 241). Yet it seems clear that, as products of the imagination, all three kinds of ethereal things need shaping under the force of intense emotion. Sperry's analysis recognizes that creativity always requires "a greeting of the Spirit." Keats's ranking, he says, suggests various ways of viewing the creative process: at one extreme ("Nothings"), Keats sees the process as "chiefly individual and reflexive," a "kind of superior amusement," and, at the other ("Things real") as "permanent and universal, a form of spiritual validation." The three kinds of beauty, therefore, may be distinguished by "various degrees of connection with (or abstraction from) material reality" (pp. 68–69). Sperry's analysis is sound, but to measure Keats's three categories by "degrees of abstraction from the concrete" is misleading unless "concrete" is carefully defined. Keats can hardly mean that, as we move upward in his scale, an external object dominates the imaginative coalescence more and more at the expense of the mind's contribution—that, for instance, either writing or reading "passages of Shakespeare" calls for a diminished contribution of thought and feeling. "Sun Moon & Stars," and "Clouds" are only metaphors for degrees of permanence. It takes imagination to give reality even to heavenly bodies. All poetry, Keats thought, must use concrete particulars; but he is saying, I think, that in etherealizing "Things real" the poet uses concrete particulars which, *through their richness of association,* provide a more substantial linking between the mind (of both poet and reader) and the world outside the poem. It is in this way, as Hazlitt argues, that death's grinning "horrible a ghastly smile" in *Paradise Lost* links the reader with the external world more closely than death's "grinning for a wager" in West's painting (18:138). Both details are concrete, but the former, being richer in shared association, thrusts the imagination toward the sublime and its essential truth. But, as Sperry asserts, in the letter of 13 March Keats's emphasis is on the "ardent pursuit" that, for any level of reality, may dignify objects and make them "Great." In this passage Keats is finding reality at that "point of thought [which] is the centre of . . . [each Man's] intellectual world" (1:243), even though its anchoring points in general experience may be relatively few.

2

Keats, however, was looking for a kind of truth which the process of sublimation could refine still more completely from a residue of self—in other words, a kind of truth more comprehensive of general experience. Although it was a "depth of speculation" which he relied on, in December 1817, to "bury repulsiveness," it is "widening speculation" which he cites in May 1818 as easing "the Burden of the Mystery" (1:277). During his most creative years he became more determined to widen as well as deepen his own speculations and so to resolve even pain and suffering into the truth that is beauty.

In Keats's letters the word *speculation* means, in its most general sense, simply mental activity, frequently conjectural. In one occurrence it means a commercial venture (2:226). More often it is loosely equivalent to "thinking" or "reasoning," although not of the "consequitive" variety. Speculation is not knowledge, but it is widened by knowledge. It is not abstract reasoning, for it coalesces "knowledge" with "high

143

Sensations" (1:277). It may involve association (1:246). It is the pleasant result of the "poetical Character's" identification with an Iago as well as an Imogen (1:387). The speculative mind is the active, ardent mind of poetic pursuit (2:80). In other words, used in relation to poetry, *speculation* becomes fairly specific, sounding very much like another term for the imagination or its product—the truth that is also beautiful.[13] Therefore, when Keats writes of "a momentous depth of speculation," he means a process or a product that by definition pleases (see also 2:77).

Among others, Addison, Gerard, Alison, Knight, and Hazlitt had agreed that extended trains of associated ideas enrich aesthetic experience with images, thought, and feeling and thus make it more enjoyable. In his copy of Hazlitt's *Characters of Shakespear's Plays*, published earlier in 1817 and probably read by Keats before writing the negative capability letter, Keats underlined a number of passages including the following:

> If there is anything in any author like this yearning of the heart, these throes of tenderness, this profound expression of all that can be thought and felt in the most heart-rending situations, we are glad of it; but it is in some author we have not read. (4:268)
>
> . . . the extremest resources of the imagination are called in to lay open the deepest movements of the heart. . . . (4:268)
>
> The greatness of Lear is not in corporal dimension, but in intellectual; the explosions of his passions are terrible as a volcano: they are storms turning up and disclosing the bottom of that rich sea, his mind, with all its vast riches. (4:271; quoted by Hazlitt from Lamb)[14]

In all three passages Hazlitt describes the intense passion of tragedy extending the imagination to bring into play reserves of thought and feeling in what he elsewhere calls "sublime aggregation." This "widening speculation" is pleasant not merely because it exercises the mind but because it reaches the level of truth accessible only to the "most impassioned species of poetry."[15]

144

Keats evidently agreed. But he is more precise than Hazlitt in distinguishing levels of truth leading to this height. In his scale of the "real," the "semireal," and "Nothings," he designates kinds of reality according to the extent that association links ethereal things with the sensory world as it is known to others. In his later letters, however, beyond or above these "halfseeings" Keats is looking for a fourth level of *whole knowledge,* toward which poetry may strive. On 24 April 1818, he wrote Taylor:

> I find that I can have no enjoyment in the World but continual drinking of Knowledge—I find there is no worthy pursuit but the idea of doing some good for the world—some do it with their society—some with their wit—some with their benevolence—some with a sort of power of conferring pleasure and good humour on all they meet . . .—there is but one way for me—the road lies th[r]ough application study and thought. I will pursue it and to that end purpose retiring for some years. I have been hovering for some time between an exquisite sense of the luxurious and a love for Philosophy—were I calculated for the former I should be glad—but as I am not I shall turn all my soul to the latter. (1:271)

In his Chamber-of-Maiden-Thought letter of 3 May 1818 to Reynolds, Keats recognizes the wholeness of knowledge and, again, the power of knowledge to relieve doubts and fears. "Every department of knowledge we see excellent and calculated towards a great whole. . . . An extensive knowledge is needful to thinking people—it takes away the heat and fever; and helps, by widening speculation, to ease the Burden of the Mystery" (1:277). Keats is thinking of knowledge combined, as in poetry, with "high Sensations" to "fledge" our shoulders so that "we go thro' the same air and space without fear." In the same letter, having described the "Chamber of Maiden-Thought" with the pleasant wonders it first opens to the mind, Keats looks into the dark passages of "Misery and Heartbreak, Pain, Sickness and oppression" leading from it, and resolves to "explore them" for their "ballance of good and evil" (1:281). To see tragedy truly and fearlessly will take a wider knowledge than Keats has yet attained.

On 19 March 1819, in his long journal letter of 14 February–3 May to George and Georgiana, Keats comes back to his correlative problems of reaching whole knowledge and doing good for the world. He himself, he says, is "pursueing the same instinctive course as the veriest human animal you can think of—I am however young writing at random—straining at particles of light in the midst of a great darkness —without knowing the bearing of any one assertion of any one opinion." Here Keats is making two points about "speculation" that he has made before about poetry: (1) its dependence on the energies of instinctive pursuit and (2) its contentment with half-knowledge. These distinguish poetry from philosophy, which calls for greater "disinterestedness" than poetry and which, not written at random, does reconcile assertions and opinions. Poetry is fine in its energy, but it "is not so fine a thing as philosophy—For the same reason that an eagle is not so fine a thing as a truth" (2:78–81). Here Keats has found his fourth level of reality: philosophy, which is integrated knowledge not, seemingly, in need of instinctive pursuit to dignify it and make it great. From "nothings" to the "real" Keats has seen poetry rising in objectivity as the poet's loss of self in identification with others enlarges a network of shared associations. Now, to top this kind of reality with "a truth," Keats has relied on another kind of selflessness —that is, on active pursuit of the good of others.

In the same letter, but six days earlier, Keats is again thinking of the distinction between poetry and the principles of thought that serve the greatest good. With admiration he quotes almost two pages from Hazlitt's *Letter to William Gifford*, including the following:

> Poetry [says Hazlitt, and] the imagination, generally speaking, delights in power, in strong excitement, as well as in truth, in good, in right, whereas pure reason and the moral sense approve only of the true and good. I proceed to show that this general love or tendency to immediate excitement or theatrical effect, no matter how produced, gives a Bias to

the imagination often [in]consistent with the greatest good, that in Poetry it triumphs over Principle, and bribes the passions to make a sacrifice of common humanity. (2:74–75; Hazlitt, 9:37)

This passage expresses Hazlitt's egalitarianism. In his essay on *Coriolanus* Hazlitt had written that "the love of power in ourselves and the admiration of it in others are both natural to man: the one makes him a tyrant, the other a slave. . . . The whole dramatic moral of *Coriolanus* is that those who have little shall have less, and that those who have much shall take all that others have left" (4:215–16). Accused by Gifford of slandering Shakespeare, Hazlitt was replying. Keats knew all these circumstances (2:74), and, we can assume, neither he nor Hazlitt would have raised a similar objection to the strong emotions in *Lear*; but it seems worth noting that, six days before he decided that an eagle and a truth are different, Keats chose to quote this particular passage from the long letter to Gifford (forty-seven closely printed pages in Howe's edition). Quite likely Hazlitt's strictures on a biased imagination reinforced—or perhaps even suggested—Keats's elevation of "a truth" beyond the ardor of pursuit.

Contrasted to poetry as "an eagle" alive and vigorous in all its power, "a truth" may appear to be only the skeleton of a whole man, a set of propositions tied together by deductive reasoning. But for Keats this is hardly the case. He did not deny philosophy the reality of experience in all its sensory as well as intellectual dimensions (1:279; 2:81),[16] nor did he think that poetry, despite its intensity, could not be philosophical. The break between an eagle and a truth does not remain as sharp as Keats's emphasis on 19 March makes it appear: at least under proper conditions an eagle can soar close to a truth. Keats's prime examples of disinterestedness are Socrates and Jesus (2:80), who after all are reported to have spoken—with ardor—a language not readily distinguishable from that of poetry. But Socrates' and Jesus' ardor was not as narrowly "instinctive" or so content with half-knowledge as a poet's might be. Keats himself wanted to be a philosophical poet. When on 9 June 1819 he wrote, "I hope

I am a little more of a Philosopher than I was, consequently a little less of a versifying Pet-lamb" (2:116), he was planning not to give up poetry but to write a different kind of poetry, more comprehensive and dealing, as he says in the "Ode on Indolence," with "visions for the night." Keats was aware that communication of knowledge from nature to man and from man to man always leaves room for error, both because the mind must select its perceptions from an otherwise un-differentiated mass of phenomena and because no two minds can make exactly the same contribution to the act of perception. The poet, therefore, must content himself with half-knowledge—that is, with not pretending, to himself or others, that he possesses full knowledge. Nevertheless, Keats hoped to organize his own knowledge more comprehensively, enrich his poetry with a wider range of common associations, and so push closer to "a truth."

The need for widening knowledge, for whole knowledge, for searching out the dark passages, and for doing all this through an integrative act of the imagination shows up further in Keats's process of "Soul-making." Again in the journal letter of spring 1819, a month after he had distinguished philosophy from poetry, Keats offers his explanation of salvation achieved through knowledge. Keats, like Hazlitt, saw no possibility of any order, political or providential, that offers mankind an escape from suffering: Keats shared both Hazlitt's championship of human rights and his lack of confidence in social amelioration as a means of freeing man from pain. Keats would not believe in perfectibility achieved through any philosophical system; nor, along with "the misguided and superstitious," would he consider the world " 'a vale of tears' from which we are to be redeemed by a certain arbitrary interposition of God and taken to Heaven—" Instead he would call the world "the vale of Soul-making," wherein "Intelligence" becomes "a Soul" through confronting "a World of Pains and troubles." This is

> a grander system of salvation than the chryst[e]ain religion— or rather it is a system of Spirit-creation—This is effected by three grand materials acting the one upon the other for a

series of years—These three Materials are the *Intelligence*— the *human heart* (as distinguished from intelligence or Mind) and the *World* or *Elemental space* suited for the proper action of *Mind and Heart* on each other for the purpose of forming the *Soul* or *Intelligence destined to possess the sense of Identity.*

Here is the coalescence of subject (intelligence and heart) and object (the world or elemental space) achieved by the imagination but attaining the mature richness or grandeur worthy to be called a "Soul" only after years in the "World of Pains and troubles." This world provides the "provings and alterations and perfectionings" that give to intelligence the "Identity" that makes it a "Soul" (2:101–103; see also 2: 79). By "salvation" Keats does not mean any sort of personal survival after death. He means attaining an identity which, although achieved by accepting process in the time-space world, resists its erosion. This, obviously, is not the identity which the "poetical Character" must surrender. It is not the identity of selfhood, which stands in the way of identification with others and sublime insights, but the identity of self-realization, in which all the powers of the mind cooperate in the creative act of the imagination. Losing the identity of selfhood is necessary to reaching the identity of self-realization. The mind must keep itself empathically open to the full process of human life, with all its pain and suffering, while the imagination takes charge and brings moral chaos into order. If, in this imaginative act, a person "survives" the process of decay and death, it is only by finding in the coalescence of his thought and feeling with sensory phenomena an organization—a set of values—superior to "the ballance of good and evil" seen in the quantitative world of time and space. It is in this organization, as distinguished from the disorder that the imagination has surmounted, that the disagreeables become agreeable.

3

Probably all of Keats's major poems as well as some of

his minor ones try to balance good and evil more satisfactorily than the material world can manage and thus to evaporate the disagreeables of destructive process. To look at all of these poems would be both impractical within the limits of this chapter and too repetitive of others' analyses. But the odes and *The Fall of Hyperion* are especially useful in showing how Keats sought to raise pain above moral disorder. "The theme of all Keats's odes except 'Psyche,' " Bate points out, "is that of process, and either the acceptance of it, or the hope to escape from it, or both in dramatic interplay with each other" (p. 512). The dramatic interplay is also between order and disorder—that is, between the truth that is beauty and the truth that is ugliness. However ordered physical changes may appear to be on the coordinates of time and space, they are none the less morally disordered in their relentless destruction of all living forms. Short of death, there is no escape from process, yet to surrender to process is to surrender to death. Process, then, must be acknowledged or accepted—not passively (for that is to die) but passionately in an act of the imagination that frees the mind from the destructive residue of time and space by measuring time qualitatively rather than quantitatively. In other words, time must be measured in its sublime rather than its material dimensions. Only in this way can man achieve an identity of understanding and action, aspiration and accomplishment, that has any kind of stability.

In stanza four of the "Ode to a Nightingale" the speaker turns successfully to Poesy as a means of escaping a painful, limited world; but after his brief, moonlit identification with the nightingale, the bird is gone and darkness closes in. Although, in stanza five, in the scant light blown down from heaven, the speaker cannot see the flowers at his feet, his still-kindled imagination enables him to grasp in clear detail the "fast-fading violets" as well as the "coming musk-rose." In the feeling of the moment, decay and growth have become part of beauty. The speaker has not, as he wished, managed to "fade far away" from the processes of time and space; instead he has confronted them and made them his own. In this imaginative act he has both accepted process and achieved identity as a creator. Of course, this identity is immediately threatened, and the poem ends with the speaker doubting which is real—the "waking dream" of the imagination or lostness in time and space. The "Ode on a Grecian Urn" resumes the search for an ordered permanence. The urn itself is simply part of the time-space world and subject to the same process of decay as any piece of well-kept marble. But it stimulates the imagination as Keats makes it "tease us out of thought / As doth eternity." The kind of thought we are teased out of is the Lockean variety, which directs mental activity to the time-space world. Keats translates the urn's power into mounting oxymoronic tensions that break down the boundaries of this world.[17] Thrust into creativity, the imagination seizes the essential beauty that is beyond temporal decay and therefore beyond time. In the third stanza of the "Ode on Melancholy" the poet again demands more than the mere observation of process; as the reader is asked to share the pain that can come only with fulfillment, the poem becomes an invitation to measure time according to the fullness of experience. Joy must be experienced before it can "bid adieu"; "aching Pleasure" cannot be unsought pleasure; only a "strenuous tongue" can "burst Joy's grape." This ode, like the "Nightingale" and the "Grecian Urn," submits process to the imagination—in this case, a more energetic imagination. In the "Ode on Indolence," when the poet-speaker bids his "Three Ghosts" adieu, the "Poesy" that he has turned away might receive a facile acclaim, but it is as out of touch with reality as the other two ghosts—all three of them but "masque-like figures on the dreamy urn." The three figures, although summarily dismissed, have brought the poet out of his benumbed indolence. He has replaced his numbness and his dreams, which after all were uneasy, with "visions for the night." His denial of process has been reversed into the ordering of process, with all its dark reality, in the creation of poetry. "To Autumn" acknowledges process throughout. The dramatic interplay is not between escaping and accepting process but between the correlatives of process itself: loss and fulfillment. This is Keats's answer to the question posed at the end of the "Nightingale." Obviously, neither loss nor fulfillment is a dream. In organizing the reality that transcends time and space, the imagination attains fulfillment only through knowing loss.

Keats, we have seen, at various times recognizes the limitations of the imagination in seizing as beauty a whole truth in a painful world. There are stubborn compounds of ugliness and evil that resist the sublimating heat of passion. We have only to return to the "Ode on a Grecian Urn" to see that Keats continued to face the problems of the imagination's limits and its contentment with halfseeing. The imaginative act which the urn has teased us into sets its own limits: it cannot admit certain ugly realities. The never-bare trees, the sweetness of unheard melodies, the persistence of unconsummated love come into sharp contrast, at the end of the third stanza, with "breathing human passion." "Happy love" may be more agreeable than the surfeit suggested by "a heart high sorrowful and cloy'd," but it falls short of the fulfillment likewise implied; and if the happiness of the lover can never be sorrow, neither can it attain the high sorrow of tragedy. The urn itself returns the imagination from order to disorder. In stanza four it looks forward and backward in time—to the "green altar" the procession is headed for and to the "little town" it has left. The town, "for evermore . . . silent . . . and . . . desolate," is emptied by the day's ceremony and, we know, long since by death. The procession leads the imagination out of the urn's ordered beauty, so that in stanza five the urn becomes only a marble "shape"—a "Cold Pastoral!" Yet, for its power to join with the viewer to create beauty and truth it remains a friend to the wasting generations in all their "woe." To be sure, the urn (as distinguished from the poem) is in no sense a tragic drama. Its truth is the kind that art supplies, but in this case its truth does not embrace the span of human experience that a tragic drama can bring into the permanence of order.

4

Keats was turning to a form of poetry in which the "World of Pains and trouble" would be felt more directly through characters caught up in it and in which the ordering force of beauty would embrace them, their evil, and their suffering. Tragedy epitomizes soul-making. The "years," says Hazlitt, "are melted down to moments" as the "human soul is made the sport of fortune, the prey of adversity [and] stretched on the wheel of destiny, in endless ecstasy" (5:51). On 14 August 1819 Keats hoped eventually "to make as great a revolution in modern dramatic writing as Kean has done in acting" (2:139). The tragedy of *Otho the Great,* written with Charles Armitage Brown in the summer of 1819, hardly qualifies. The story seems to have been Brown's invention, with Keats doing little more than versifying the first four acts but, in Act V, working as independently as the first four acts would let him. King Otho's son Ludolph, who dominates Act V, fails to organize his tragic world in any very mature way before he goes mad and, along with his faithless bride, dies of accumulated tensions. *King Stephen,* which probably followed close upon *Otho,* is all Keats's own. This fragment discloses a growing mastery of dramatic action, but its little more than two hundred lines are not enough to demonstrate how Keats would have handled the disagreeables.[18]

Although Keats never wrote a tragedy of his own, the two fragmentary *Hyperions* show his growing commitment to tragedy. Keats wrote most of *Hyperion* in the autumn of 1818 and began *The Fall of Hyperion* in July 1819. In the intervening months he had written his long letter of 14 February–3 May to the George Keatses—with its speculations on disinterestedness, philosophy, and soul-making—and all the odes except "To Autumn." Both *Hyperions* deal with the fall of the Titans in a manner reminiscent of Milton's fallen angels; both seem about to center on the threatened fall of the sun-god Hyperion; and both describe a poet acquiring knowledge from a fallen goddess. Keats apparently intended character and action—especially, one would think, the character and actions of Hyperion—to organize the reality that gets the better of destructive process. In the fragments that Keats has left us, Hyperion has not reached any solution to his problems, and whether or not he ever could have is a question that has been discussed a good deal. In *Hyperion,* as the fallen gods debate, Oceanus has settled matters to his own satisfaction, but his dispassionate acceptance of the new order's "fresh perfection" does not reach tragic proportions (canto 2, ll. 173ff.), while Enceladus's rebelliousness promises nothing but inevitable surrender.

For something more closely resembling a tragic resolution we may look at the dialogs between Mnemosyne and Apollo in *Hyperion* and Moneta and the dreamer-poet in *The Fall of Hyperion.* Keats had come to the conclusion, which we have noted in his letters, that in order to evaporate the ugliest disagreeables the passions could not be "in their sublime" without an intellectual force derived from "extensive knowledge." In *Hyperion* the deliberate pace of the god-making process in yielding up knowledge causes Apollo considerable anguish; but, although the historical information he finally reads in Mnemosyne's face may be "enormous," we have to take Apollo's word for his resulting deification. The connection between creative passion and "Names, deeds, grey legends, [and] dire events" is not shown dramatically. Written a year later, *The Fall of Hyperion* returns to disinterestedness and knowledge as correlative means of widening speculation and elevating it above the disorder of time and space. The dialog between Moneta and the dreamer deals with both of these themes and dramatizes the dreamer's search for knowledge more successfully than the earlier conversation between Mnemosyne and Apollo. Keats brings Moneta's tragic knowledge home to the imagination.

The widening of Keats's own knowledge—in the sense that knowledge is something derived from reading—is well illustrated in *The Fall of Hyperion.* Keats's assimilation of the Bible, Egyptian and Druidic religions, Greek and Roman antiquity, Hesiod, Ovid, Dante, Milton, and others has been searched out.[19] The purpose of this analysis is not to repeat that search but to show the importance that Keats attached to widened speculation and the disinterestedness necessary to it as a means of evaporating the tragic disagreeables. *The Fall of Hyperion* takes the form of a dream vision patterned after the *Purgatorio*. The dreamer approaches the shrine of Moneta, who is the memory and embodiment of Man's tragic past (canto 1, ll. 87ff.). The veiled Moneta offers the dreamer alternatives of climbing the steps to her shrine or dying on "that marble" where he stands. The climb seems so formidable that he almost accepts death, but, when he finally takes the more difficult course of setting his foot on "the lowest stair," life (imaginative power?) pours into him and he ascends. Wondering why he alone has escaped from death, he asks Moneta why those "thousands in the world . . . / Who love their fellows . . . / And . . . / Labour for mortal good" are absent from the shrine. The goddess's reply recalls Keats's distinction between his and others' ways of doing good (1: 271). Unlike the dreamer, says Moneta, these practical humanists are not "vision'ries," or "dreamers weak," of dubious value to the world. They go about their work seeking "no wonder but the human face." Furthermore, among those who do enter her fane, Moneta distinguishes between those who "rot on the pavement" and those who, like the dreamer, only "half-rot" before ascending to the shrine. The latter so feel the "miseries of the world" that, unable to separate joy from pain, they cannot rest (canto 1, ll. 147–63). By mounting the steps the dreamer has shown Moneta that he is not among the "thoughtless" who "find a haven in the world / . . . [to] sleep away their days," but apparently, in a passage Woodhouse says that Keats intended to omit (canto 1, ll. 187–210), the dreamer still has not convinced Moneta that his restlessness under the world's misery is not just a form of self-pity.

> "Art thou not of the dreamer tribe?
> The poet and the dreamer are distinct. . . .
> The one pours out a balm upon the World,
> The other vexes it." (Canto 1, ll. 197–202)

The dreamer protests; but since Moneta is not a goddess likely to be persuaded by mere vehemence, the dreamer's ascent to her shrine probably had already convinced her of his serious and disinterested purpose.[20] At any rate, when she finally parts her veils, the dreamer proves himself to be a poet as his imagination seizes as beautiful the tragedy that her face reveals. Hers is

> a wan face,
> Not pin'd by human sorrows, but bright-blanch'd
> By an immortal sickness which kills not;
> It works a constant change, which happy death
> Can put no end to; deathwards progressing
> To no death was that visage; it had past
> The lilly and the snow. . . . (Canto 1, ll. 256–62)

The poet would have fled; only Moneta's eyes hold him back

> with a benignant light,
> Soft mitigated by divinest lids
> Half-closed, and visionless entire they seem'd
> Of all external things. (Canto 1, ll. 265–68)

In Moneta's face the poet reads both the wasting pain of death and man's never-ending endurance of it. Here the time-denying oxymorons, unlike those in the "Grecian Urn," bear directly on pain and suffering. We are pushed toward the eternal, not by unheard melodies or loveless love, but by immortal sickness and death-bound deathlessness. The poet's knowledge, unlike that which Apollo reads in Mnemosyne's face, is fused with "high Sensations" and thus in the sublime intensity of the moment translated out of the boundaries of time and space.

"Adorant at her feet," the poet begs to know "what high tragedy / In the dark secret chambers of her skull" could bring

> so dread a stress
> To her cold lips, and fill with such a light
> Her planetary eyes; and touch her voice
> With such a sorrow. . . . (Canto 1, ll. 277–83)

Her answer is a simple one, given as the poet glimpses the fallen Titans sitting motionless beneath "the gloomy boughs." "So Saturn sat," Moneta answers, "When he had lost his Realms—" (canto 1, ll. 297–302). As both Hazlitt and Keats recognized in the tragedies of Shakespeare, the dramatic form marks the completest unselfing that a poet can attain—the ultimate triumph of the "poetical Character."[21] As Moneta turns to the figures of Saturn and Thea, the poet recognizes and shares, in his sympathy with outward forms, the imagination's climactic unselfing. Within him there grows

> A power . . . of enormous ken
> To see as a god sees, and take the depth
> Of things as nimbly as the outward eye
> Can size and shape pervade. (Canto 1, ll. 303–306)

Keats describes the large and penetrating process of the imagination that he and Hazlitt termed sublime. Keats has projected the immediate perception of essence to a tragic view of life. The poet in *The Fall of Hyperion* has resolved his problem. In this version of the Biblical and Miltonic myth of fall and redemption, the poet has expiated "the original Sin in Poetry" described by Hazlitt in the passage Keats quoted from the *Letter to Gifford* as "bribing the passions to make a sacrifice of humanity" or explained in Keats's terms as the self-indulgence of instinctively pursuing only half-knowledge rather than disinterestedly looking for whole knowledge.[22] In March 1819 Keats had questioned, as Sperry points out, whether in following his "instinctive course" he might not be "free from sin" (2:80), but now his ardor is no longer centered at the shifting point of his own self-centered pursuits. With the disinterested concern for good that alone can push poetry above the "real" toward the greater objectivity of philosophic truth, Keats has widened his speculation to balance good and evil. He has seen evil as well as good submissive to the purifying power of sublime passion, and he has thus regarded pain and suffering in its eternal truth.

 The Fall of Hyperion ends without showing precisely how, in character and action, the poet will use his empathic insight, and the knowledge of suffering that it is supposed to bring him, to pour "a balm upon the world." The poet discovers that passion in its sublime power to evaporate the disagreeables cannot be sustained.

> Without stay or prop,
> But my own weak mortality, I bore
> The load of this eternal quietude,
> The unchanging gloom, and the fixed shapes
> Ponderous upon my senses, a whole moon.
> (Canto 1, ll. 388–92)

The situation remains unresolved: the Titans only sit and wait while the doomed Hyperion flares on. Keats did not live to write the tragic drama in which the interplay of character and action might have evaporated the disagreeables in the emergence of identity. Had he written his tragedy, almost certainly he would have tried to dramatize "the fierce dispute / Betwixt damnation and impassion'd clay" which he had to "burn through" as he sat down to read *King Lear* once again. Under the stress of tragic action, character would have achieved order wrested out of disorder—a kind of permanence painfully wrought from process and realized in images reflecting mankind's eternal confrontation of pain. This orderly truth—like the poet's vision of Moneta's face—would embrace suffering and evil, translating it from the disagreeable into the high-sorrowful beauty of fulfillment.

CHAPTER TEN

"THE FIERCE DISPUTE"

For Dennis, Hazlitt, and Keats, the sublime brings knowledge and emotion together to evaporate the tragic disagreeables. Psychologically Dennis's process of evaporation is much like Hazlitt's and Keats's: association fuses imagery with thought and feeling so that its immediate impact on the reader produces not only intense emotion but, stimulated by that emotion, a rational cognition of truth. There are, to be sure, important differences. For Dennis, the imagination is only an imaging faculty, its images being combined and harmonized under the direction of reason. For Hazlitt and Keats, it is the imagination that unifies all the faculties in the creative act. For Dennis, reason is a superior faculty that can reach beyond sensation, logic, and analysis to a direct insight into truth. Hazlitt and Keats stay within the epistemology of Hobbes and Locke but believe that habitual and thoughtful experience may condition the imagination to discern a higher and more permanent kind of truth than that available to mere logic and analysis. Furthermore, Dennis finds sublimity only in the epic and in "the greater Ode." Before the sublime could bring knowledge as well as feeling to bear on the pain and suffering of tragedy, both the imagination and the sublime had to undergo a century of change.

1

Addison, like Dennis, makes imagination an imaging faculty, but he breaks up the partnership of imagination and reason. Judgment maintains the minor role of comparing the representation with the original and thus offering a kind of knowledge; but the ultimate truths of God's universe and man's place therein may be approached only by intellectual powers that Addison leaves out of the aesthetic experience. Thus Addison makes a firm distinction between (1) aesthetic experience, as involving the understanding to a very limited degree at best, and (2) the enlargement of knowledge that ultimately requires deductive reasoning. The pleasurable effects of greatness—and, for that matter, of beauty and novelty—are principally emotional. After Addison the imagination had to supply new insights before the sublime could once again, as it does in Dennis, convert the terrors of human life into pleasures both emotionally and intellectually satisfying.

Addison recognizes that trains of associated ideas can make the secondary pleasures of the imagination richer and more intense than primary ones, but he sees their contribution as little more than emotion. Burke makes imagination only a substitute for sensation. He can allow the sublime or the beautiful an emotional impact but not any intellectual component. Gerard permits his trains a wider mental scope, but he switches them away from the upper realms of intellectual activity, which are reserved for reason. When it comes to finding the truth, imagination is still in an inferior position. Alison makes room in the trains for all the operations of the mind, but in applying his aesthetic to tragedy, he still limits the cognitive range of art. Knight, although he distinguishes aesthetic from practical experience and gives association an important role in forming sublime ideas, remains a follower of Burke by confining tragic pleasure to sympathetic emotion.

It was not until the early nineteenth century that the full intellectual power of the associating process would be applied in the practical criticism of tragedy.

Partly as a result of the expanding process of the imagination, the sublime also underwent some changes from Addison to Alison. Addison finds greatness in "the Largeness of a whole view, considered as one entire piece" (*Spectator* 412). Inherent in this visual bulk is power, the power of an infinite God and the power felt by the viewer as he responds to magnitude and its supernatural implications. Alison retains the magnitude and power of sublimity, but, although recognizing the importance of visual detail, he breaks sublimity free from the visual integrity insisted on by Addison, Baillie, and—sometimes—Gerard. Addison, Baillie, Burke, Gerard, Knight, and others all attribute sublime feelings *directly* to ideas rather than objects. They also acknowledge that these ideas may be formed from a wide range of "objects" not in themselves large but suggesting feelings associated with magnitude. But all of these ideas are still dominated by visual qualities and the pleasures ascribed to them, often a more-or-less vague feeling of providential power or a feeling of excitement pleasant for its own sake. In Alison's trains of associated ideas, however, physical size with visual integrity is replaced by psychological size with emotional integrity. Alison's sublime requires a large and emotionally unified aggregation of ideas pleasurable in the process of accumulation rather than in its ultimate resemblance to a large and spatially unified object. For Alison, therefore, the sublime readily becomes a quality of dramatic as well as nondramatic poetry.

As psychologically rather than only spatially large, the sublime could deal with more painful disagreeables. As a property inhering in large objects, the sublime offered a pleasant suggestion of God's infinitude. Thus Addison's "greatness" could overcome, with a feeling of God's power, the unpleasantness of rude landscapes. The sublime, even more than other aesthetic experiences, could also overcome unpleasant ennui by some mind-expanding exercise, analogous

161

to the physical effort of traversing a considerable amount of space. But these pleasures were regarded as inferior in quality to those of reason. This separation of mind-stretching from knowing did not exist in Dennis; and it was only when the cognitive process and a different kind of mind-stretching process were identified with each other, as they were in Alison, that the sublime was once more ready to take on the ultimate disagreeableness of evil. In other words, the mind-stretching had to become the psychological process of wide-ranging, deeply probing association: a flux of imagery and thought that measures time and space by quality, not quantity. Addison describes the process in a rudimentary way but allows it to evaporate only the "little Disagreeableness" of ugly visual details. Burke removes Addison's and Baillie's distinction between the sublime and the pathetic and thus identifies the sublime with tragedy, but he does not allow art any unique power to deal with the tragic disagreeables. Tragedy simply offers the same raw stimulus to feeling as an actual hanging might. Gerard gives aesthetic experience its own kind of control over the disagreeables, and he brings his trains of ideas to bear on a wider range of disagreeables than Addison does. He shows how moral shocks can be converted to add to the total pleasure of a work of art. But the dichotomy persists. The pleasures of taste are inferior to those of reason. The cognitive power of association, unable to engage the higher faculties, must have its pleasures supplemented by the noncognitive mind-stirring attributed to sizable objects. Knight also refines and extends the power of the imagination and frees tragedy from much of the crude emotionalism that spread from the affective hypothesis, but his sublime pleasures of tragedy are still limited to those of the visible sublime. Alison, however, freed the sublime from the tyranny of physical magnitude, allowing it to offer pleasures no longer spatially restricted. In other words, he opened the way to the sublime of vision, which results when the imagination, stimulated by sensory particulars, combines all the resources of the mind to organize reality. Yet, in his brief comments on tragedy, Alison still does not see tragedy as confronting evil

162

intellectually. His sublime is better able to deal with geo-
logic monstrosity than with moral upheavals.

Romantic criticism, however, uses the imagination to
turn the whole force of the mind on the problem of evil. For
Hazlitt and Keats, as for Dennis, the sublime harmonizes the
faculties in self-fulfilling mental activity that is exciting and,
in its excitement, fully cognitive. It is in the nature of this
creative act to come to terms with evil. But Hazlitt's and
Keats's terms are different from Dennis's. For Dennis, evil
loses its disagreeableness when its place in the divine order is
recognized. This recognition may come immediately through
an idea expanded in "meditation" or through deduction
from a moral fable. In either case, reason takes a part. Had
Dennis written his promised analysis of "Compassion and
Terror" in tragedy, he might also have expanded tragic characters (like the lions and the tigers) into symbols of universal
will, even though he almost certainly would have insisted on
a moral fable as well. In any case, the creative act, as well as
its counterpart for the audience, would bring man's will into
accord with the will of God as revealed by the moral effects
of pity and fear as well as by the distribution of justice. In
defining the world of tragedy as a moral chaos brought into
order only by the human mind, Hazlitt and Keats reject any
divine regulation. Their inheritance from the "affective
hypothesis" of Burke and others is not only an emphasis on
sympathetic feeling and therefore character, but also a denial
of tragedy as demonstration. Their definition of tragedy—of
any kind of poetry, in fact—rejects demonstrable propositions
as abstract and therefore unable to express reality. All systems of thought—philosophic, religious, political, economic
—suffer from abstraction. Such systems stand in the way of
truth that must be discovered, in all its multiplicity and
fluidity, by keeping the mind open to the continual flow of
sensation, thought, and feeling. Truth resides in this dynamic
flux as the trains of ideas collect and merge the resources of
the mind. If the imagination is to attain the highest order
of truth, these resources must include a network of associations drawn from broad, thoughtful, and sympathetic expe-

rience. Both Hazlitt and Keats recognize that the sublime of vision must transcend idiosyncrasy. Hazlitt explains the associational process of vision more fully than Keats, but Keats goes further than Hazlitt in specifying the intellectual dimensions that withstand erosion by time and space. Hazlitt and Keats agree that tragedy, more than any other kind of poetry, extends this process and these dimensions.

In giving tragedy this high place among the poetic genres, Hazlitt and Keats broke both with Dennis and with those of their contemporaries who found the epic and the Scriptures uniquely sublime. For Wordsworth, Coleridge, and De Quincey, sublimity was a religious emotion distinct from the pleasures of beauty. On the other hand, without diminishing its emotional power, Blake, Shelley, Hunt, Hazlitt, and Keats secularized the sublime. What Harold Bloom has called the "displaced Protestantism" of Romantic poetry claimed even the theater for sublimity.[1] It was rarely to the poets of their own age, however, that Romantic critics turned for tragedies that could arouse the most elevated passions.

2

Disaster has never been a popular commodity. Yet, in their myths, some cultures have faced up to its threat more boldly than others, whereas "declining cultures," Geoffrey Brereton finds, "are afraid of being hurt and are inclined to take refuge in petty repetition and unadventurous didacticism."[2] Eighteenth-century Britain produced no great tragedy, and neither did the Romantic Period. The "epoch of concentration" that Matthew Arnold describes as following the French Revolution produced only, as a rebuke to concentration, great criticism of the tragedies of an earlier age. What Arnold calls "all these fine ideas of the reason" underlying the French Revolution had lost their creative force as they were trimmed down to meet the practical needs of the Industrial Revolution.[3] In early nineteenth-century England the myth of progress—with its promise of material rewards for all if everyone is free to act on a calculation of consequences to his own welfare—had already taken form; and it was against the narrow rationalism and self-interest implicit in this myth that Blake, Coleridge, Wordsworth, Shelley, Hazlitt, Keats, and others shaped their definitions of imagination. The empirical philosophy, descended from Hobbes and Locke and applied by Adam Smith and Malthus to the support of free enterprise, had reduced reason to analysis and logic, and morality, in effect, to self-centered prudence. Reason was no longer the comprehensive faculty which, in the Middle Ages and the Renaissance, was thought to organize the whole mind in discerning truth and directing the will. The "modern philosophy," Hazlitt and Keats believed, fractioned the mind, discouraging the imagination necessary to sympathy with others, to moral direction, and, indeed, to grasping reality in all its dimensions. At times hardly distinguishable in its practical force from the pressures of political reaction, it combined with these pressures, says Hazlitt, to divert the philosopher from truth, the statesman from comprehensive principles of political action, the poet from the wholeness of human experience, and the citizen from the full humanity that is the life of a free society.[4]

For a century and a half the myth of progress—with science as its prime mover and technology its gauge—has served up material benefits to a growing but still limited number of the world's population. Yet the force of Hazlitt's censure—and of course the censure bestowed by Coleridge, Carlyle, and many others—has scarcely diminished. The order that we have so successfully imposed on the material world leaves off at the edge of that world, beyond which disorder multiplies into new dimensions. The myths that elevate the physical as a measure of value, supported by the unfocused metaphors of popular religion, have closed the mind to some difficult parts of life which nevertheless must be confronted if we are to become complete human beings. Confrontation can never be passive. The confrontation of evil requires the whole mind brought alive by the imagination.

Only tragedy, Hazlitt and Keats believed, displays and

evokes this power of imagination at its farthest reach. Literature, of course, is not indispensable to "Soul-making." Keats's "fierce dispute" is not unique to persons with education or other privileges. But only literature can put some kinds of truth into words; and of all kinds of literature, tragedy tells the truth that flabbiness can least endure. If there is a common element in modern explanations of tragic pleasure, it is that tragedy brings home the truth: the truth of complete human experience and not an abstraction therefrom. This truth is created as the tragic character confronts —with all the intensity that this word implies—a world of pain and death, thereby more deeply penetrating the perplexities of right and wrong and bringing them into some sort of order. Even if the character's own thought does not approach the height of Hamlet's or Lear's, the play may disclose the coherence of thought itself. "The world of everyday," writes F. L. Lucas, "seems often a purposeless chaos, a mangy tiger without even the fearful symmetry of Blake's vision; but the world of tragedy we can face, for we feel a mind behind it and the symmetry is there."[5] The mind, of course, is the playwright's, evident in the collective pleasures of language, probable action, reality of character, excitement and control of emotion, and the knowledge of evil and its place in human life. According to Hazlitt and Keats, the audience attains this knowledge from tragedy by sharing the scope of thought and feeling, and the accompanying self-realization, reached by the tragic hero. As the tragic hero gains this sort of ascendancy over the evil that will destroy him, the audience or reader sublimely stretches his mind to comprehend man's capability for doing, enduring, and understanding evil.

This extended knowledge is the "conscious power" of identity achieved *in extremis*. We enjoy the power of feeling, says Hazlitt, the power of hating evil as well as loving good. But a great tragedy adds the further pleasure of knowing the thing we hate, for it turns up all the faculties to full power in fusing vast disorder into truth and beauty. This knowledge does not free man from pain or death. Tragedy offers only the freedom to achieve, by sharing the fierce dispute, the identity of self-fulfillment. A lesser confrontation will not do: only in sublime passion will the mind stretch itself to know both the enormity and the enormousness of life.

NOTES

INTRODUCTION: THE SUBLIME AND THE TRAGIC

1. See Earl R. Wasserman, "The Pleasures of Tragedy," *ELH* 4 (1947):293–307; Baxter Hathaway, "The Lucretian 'Return upon Ourselves' in Eighteenth-Century Theories of Tragedy," *PMLA* 42 (1947):672–89; Eric Rothstein, "English Tragic Theory in the Late Seventeenth Century," *ELH* 29 (1962):306–23. Rothstein's article appears, with some revision, as the first chapter of his *Restoration Tragedy* (Madison, Wis., 1967).

2. See Samuel H. Monk, *The Sublime: A Study of Critical Theories in XVIII-Century England* (Ann Arbor, Mich., 1960), p. 21; and David B. Morris, *The Religious Sublime* (Lexington, Ky., 1972).

3. See Marjorie Nicolson, *Mountain Gloom and Mountain Glory* (Ithaca, N.Y., 1959), pp. 185–270; Ernest Tuveson, "Space, Deity, and the 'Natural Sublime,'" *Modern Language Quarterly* 12 (1951):20–38; and Tuveson, *Imagination as a Means of Grace* (Berkeley, Calif., 1960), pp. 56–71. Cf. R. S. Crane's review of Monk, *The Sublime*, in *Philological Quarterly* 15 (1936):165–67; and Morris, pp. 2–9.

4. [Cassius] Longinus, *On the Sublime*, trans. B. Einarson, and

Sir Joshua Reynolds, *Discourses on Art,* with intro. by Elder Olson (Chicago, 1945), pp. 4–5, 13, 62–63 (secs. 1, 6, 35–36).

5. See Jeffry B. Spencer, *Heroic Nature* (Evanston, Ill., 1973), pp. 276–81.

6. *Life of Milton, Rasselas,* and *Preface to Shakespeare,* in *The Works of Samuel Johnson* (Oxford, 1825), 7:133–35; 1:221–22; 5:105; "Notes on Shakespeare's Plays," *Johnson on Shakespeare,* ed. Arthur Sherbo (New Haven, Conn., 1968), pp. 120, 642, 652, et passim; J. H. Hagstrum, "Johnson's Conception of the Beautiful, the Pathetic, and the Sublime," *PMLA* 44 (1949):134–57.

7. Henry Home, Lord Kames, *Elements of Criticism,* 6th ed., 2 vols. (Edinburgh, 1785), 1:217–21, 238 (chap. 4); 2:375 (chap. 22).

8. [John] Baillie, *An Essay on the Sublime* (Augustan Reprint Society: Los Angeles, 1953), p. 10.

9. R. Rapin, *Reflections on Aristotle's Treatise of Poesie* (London, 1674), pp. 104–105 (chap. 18); "Preface to *Troilus and Cressida,*" *Essays of John Dryden,* ed. W. P. Ker (New York, 1961), 1:209–10. Quoted in Rothstein, *ELH* 29:316. For Dennis, see my chap. 1, p. 22.

10. All references to *The Spectator* are to the edition ed. Donald F. Bond, 5 vols. (Oxford, 1965).

11. *An Inquiry into the Origin of Our Ideas of Beauty and Virtue,* 2d ed. (London, 1726), pp. 86, 239 (bk. 1, chap. 4; bk. 2, chap. 5).

12. See William Hazlitt, *Complete Works,* ed. P. P. Howe, 21 vols. (London, 1930–34), 2:204, 209, 215, 282; W. P. Albrecht, *Hazlitt and the Creative Imagination* (Lawrence, Kans., 1965), pp. 12–13; Leonard M. Trawick, III, "Hazlitt, Reynolds, and the Ideal," *Studies in Romanticism* 4 (1965): 240–47; Roy Park, *Hazlitt and the Spirit of the Age* (Oxford, 1971), pp. 97–99. All references to Hazlitt's writings will be to the *Complete Works.*

CHAPTER ONE: DENNIS

1. In *The Critical Works of John Dennis,* ed. Edward N. Hooker, 2 vols. (Baltimore, 1939–1943). See [Thomas Burnet], *The Sacred Theory of the Earth,* 5th ed., 2 vols. (London, 1722), 1:188–89 (bk. 1, chap. 11); 1:71–128 (bk. 1, chaps.

Notes to Pages 14–21

5, 6, 7). The first edition of *The Sacred Theory* appeared in Latin in 1681, the first English edition in 1684. See also Nicolson, *Mountain Gloom*, pp. 277–78.

2. See Morris, *Religious Sublime*, p. 60–65.
3. See also Dennis, *Works*, 1:188, 213, 217–18, 261, 264, 290, 363; Explanatory Notes, 1:489–90; Editor's Introduction, 2: xcvii–xcviii; 2:363, 383. Cf. Thomas Hobbes, *Leviathan*, ed. M. Oakeshott (Oxford, 1957), pp. 8–17, 25–27, 42–44 (bk. 1, chaps. 4, 5, 7). C. D. Thorpe, *The Aesthetic Theory of Thomas Hobbes* (Ann Arbor, Mich., 1940), pp. 221–59, examines Dennis's debt to Hobbes. Although I would agree that in Dennis as in Hobbes the perception of "the actual [sense] impression is modified by the intervention of judgment operating upon the incoming image and previous impression re-presented by memory" (pp. 229–31), I find it difficult to compare, as Thorpe does (p. 232), Hobbes's "deliberation," which is common to both men and animals (*Leviathan*, p. 37 [1. 6]), with Dennis's "meditation" (see my pp. 16–19). Miss Nicolson, who also disagrees with Thorpe in this respect, finds Dennis "much closer to the Cambridge Platonists [than to Hobbes] in every way" (pp. 281–82, n.).
4. See Dennis, *Works*, Introduction, 2:xcv–xcvii, and Explanatory Notes, 1:508, 516; Monk, *Sublime*, p. 35; Nicolson, *Mountain Gloom*, p. 288, n. See also L. A. Elioseff, *The Cultural Milieu of Addison's Criticism* (Austin, Tex., 1963), p. 102.
5. These passages are cited in Morris, *Religious Sublime*, pp. 70, 75. Cf. Scott Elledge, "The Background and Development in English Criticism of the Theories of Generality and Particularity," *PMLA* 62 (1947):162.
6. *Leviathan*, p. 43 (1. 8). See Thorpe, *Aesthetic Theory*, pp. 230–31.
7. See also above, note 3.
8. Cf. *On the Sublime*, pp. 4–5, 13–15 (secs. 1, 7, 8).
9. *Essay on the Sublime*, pp. 10–11, 23–24.
10. See Monk, *Sublime*, p. 54.
11. See also 1:159, 183–84, 200; 2:18–22.
12. Cf. Monk, *Sublime*, pp. 48–49, who seems to say that Dennis's sun illustration differentiates between vulgar and enthusiastic passions (pp. 48–49), and Morris, *Religious Sublime*, who says that "Ordinary (or Vulgar) passion results from

171

direct and immediate sensation" (p. 50). The same interpretation appears again in J. A. W. Heffernan, "Wordsworth and Dennis: The Discrimination of Feelings," *PMLA* 82 (1967):430–36: "According to Dennis, objects evoke a 'Vulgar Passion' when they affect us by powers of their own, while they elicit an 'Enthusiastick Passion' when they affect us by symbolic properties meditatively infused" (p. 432). But the evidence supports Thorpe's conclusion that "even the vulgar passions essential to poetry may be aroused by reflection" (*Aesthetic Theory*, p. 228). Heffernan seems to find a "scale" of "imaginative exertion," in both Wordsworth and Dennis, running from the "human" or "ordinary" to the "enthusiastick" or "imaginative" (pp. 432–35). This does suggest the ascending intensity of vulgar passions toward enthusiasm, but somewhere along the line there should probably be a change in kind as well as in degree.

13. The strong-excitement tradition has been explained in Cartesian and Hobbesian terms. Both Descartes and Hobbes equated passion to matter in motion initiated by external bodies. Both stated conditions for pleasurable passion: agreement with appetite (in Hobbes) and adjustment of the motion to nervous and bodily capabilities (in Descartes). See *Leviathan*, pp. 31–34 (1.6); Descartes, *Oeuvres*, 11 vols. (Paris, 1824), 4:114–16 ("Les Passions de l'âme," art. 94); and Wasserman, *ELH* 4:288–89, n. Dennis, too, makes the pleasure of passion contingent on a kind of harmony—with the will and hence with the reason (1:150–51, 263–64, et passim); but despite his frequent use of the words "move" and "motion" in describing the passions and despite his other resemblances to Hobbes, his conception of reason and its powers would rule out making him a materialist, at least a thorough-going one. See Nicolson, *Mountain Gloom*, pp. 281–82, n.

14. Rothstein, *ELH* 29:311, and 319–20.

15. [Jean-Baptiste] Du Bos, *Refléxions critique sur la poésie et sur la peinture*, 5th ed., 3 vols. (Paris, 1746), 1:5–11 (pt. 1, sec. 1). Cf. [Bernard Le Bovier de] Fontenelle, "Refléxions sur la poétique," in *Oeuvres* (Paris, 1758), 3:162–63.

16. According to Howe's index, Hazlitt mentions Dennis only four times, twice rather scornfully and twice approving his *Remarks upon Cato* for deprecating a strict observance of

the unities of time and place (*Complete Works,* 5:322; 6:89, 356; 11:318). Dennis is not listed in Rollins's index to Keats's *Letters.* Dennis won Wordsworth's approval and apparently influenced his understanding of the imagination (especially for the effect of passion); and Wordsworth's prefaces may have influenced Hazlitt. But these links are hardly strong enough to build a case on. See *The Letters of William and Dorothy Wordsworth: The Middle Years,* ed. E. de Selincourt, 2 vols. (Oxford, 1937), 2:617 (letter to Catherine Clarkson, Dec. 1814); Dennis, *Critical Works,* 2:lxxiii; Heffernan, *PMLA* 82:430–36; Thorpe, *Aesthetic Theory,* pp. 228–30.

CHAPTER TWO: ADDISON

1. *Leviathan,* pp. 9–10, 30 (1. 2, 4). As Elioseff points out in *Cultural Milieu,* p. 170, "Strictly speaking, the imagination is not a faculty at all, but represents one of the ways in which the unified soul operates. . . . Addison, however, continues to speak of the parts of the soul (memory, imagination, will, and reason) as if they were independent faculties, but this expression is a product of convenience and custom."
2. John Locke, *An Essay Concerning Human Understanding,* ed. A. C. Fraser, 2 vols. (Oxford, 1894), 2:146–47 (bk. 3, chap. 10, sec. 34).
3. All quotations from *The Spectator* are from Donald F. Bond's edition, 5 vols. (Oxford, 1965).
4. *Essay Concerning Human Understanding,* 1: esp. 168–73 (2. 8. 7–15). Light and color are what Locke calls "secondary qualities" of objects, as distinguished from "primary qualities"—such as solidity, extension, figure, and mobility—which are not "separable from the body." Obviously, this distinction bears only a very general kind of resemblance to Addison's division into primary and secondary pleasures. Cf. W. J. Hipple, Jr., *The Beautiful, the Sublime, and the Picturesque in Eighteenth-Century British Aesthetic Theory* (Carbondale, Ill., 1957), pp. 15, 324. C. D. Thorpe, "Addison's Contribution to Criticism," in Richard Foster Jones, et al., *The Seventeenth Century: Studies in the History of English Thought and Literature from Bacon to Pope* (Stanford, Calif., 1951), p. 323; and Elioseff, *Cultural Milieu,* pp. 162–69.

5. Addison's classification of aesthetic properties or effects as great, novel, and beautiful—a classification that became influential among later critics—was perhaps not entirely original. Suggestions for it have been found in both Longinus and Burnet; but Addison does not follow either of these possible sources closely, and his distinctions are clearer as well as more detailed. Like Longinus, apparently, and unlike Burnet, Addison does not make his categories mutually exclusive. "The Fancy delights in every thing that is Great, Strange, or Beautiful, and is still more pleased the more it finds these Perfections in the same object" (S. 412). See On the Sublime, p. 62 (chap. 35); [Thomas Burnet], An Answer to the Exceptions Made by Mr. Erasmus Warren against the Sacred Theory of the Earth, 3d ed. (London, 1722), p. 23 (chap 7). See also Hipple, The Beautiful, p. 16; Nicolson, Mountain Gloom, pp. 311–12 ;Elioseff, Cultural Milieu, pp. 179–80.

6. Monk, Sublime, p. 6.

7. Elioseff, Cultural Milieu, pp. 96, 97, 103, 106–107.

8. See Addison's Remarks on Several Parts of Italy, in Works, ed. G. W. Greene, 5 vols. (Philadelphia, 1876), 2:217, 268–69, 339–40; Nicolson, Mountain Gloom, pp. 303–305; and Elioseff, Cultural Milieu, p. 107.

9. The Pleasures of Imagination (bk. 1, ll. 53–73, 96–124), in The Poetical Works of Mark Akenside, ed. Alexander Dyce (London, 1894), pp. 7–9. See Robert Marsh, "Akenside and Addison: The Problem of Ideational Debt," Modern Philology 59 (1961):36–48.

10. See Essay Concerning Human Understanding, 1:418 (2. 33).

11. According to C. D. Thorpe, Addison's assignment of the imagination to "an intermediate position between sense and understanding" was especially influenced by Descartes ("Addison's Theory of the Imagination as 'Perceptive Response,'" Papers of the Michigan Academy of Science, Arts, and Letters 21[1935]:509–30).

12. See Edward A. and Lillian D. Bloom, "Addison on 'Moral Habits of the Mind,'" Journal of the History of Ideas 21 (1960):409–27.

13. See Essay Concerning Human Understanding, 2:386–87 (4. 17).

14. David Hume, A Treatise of Human Nature, ed. L. A. Selby-

Bigge, 2 vols. (London, 1896), 2:435–36 (pt. 3, sec. 8). Cf. Baillie, *Essay on the Sublime*, pp. 4–11; Alexander Gerard, *An Essay on Taste*, 3d ed. (London, 1780), p. 12 (pt. 1, sec. 2).

15. Kames, *Elements of Criticism*, 1:210–11 (chap. 4). See also 1:23 (chap. 1).

16. *The Letters of John Keats 1814–1821*, ed. Hyder E. Rollins, 2 vols. (Cambridge, Mass., 1958), 1:301.

17. Longinus also remarks on "great" bodies of water and volcanic craters pouring out "rocks and precipices" (*On the Sublime*, pp. 62–63 [secs. 35–36]), features that he may have helped contribute to Addison's description of greatness; but in the passage just quoted from *S.* 417 Addison clearly has his own earlier account of greatness (*S.* 412) in mind.

18. Cf. Descartes, *Oeuvres*, 4:56, 72 ("Les Passions de l'âme," arts. 21, 43); 4:398–403, 407–408 ("L'Homme"). For the influence of Descartes on Addison, see Nicolson, *Mountain Gloom*, pp. 302–303; Thorpe, "Addison's Theory of the Imagination," pp. 522–29.

19. David Hartley, *Observations on Man, His Frame, His Duty, and His Expectations*, 4th ed., 3 vols. (London, 1801), 1:11–12, 56, 59–61.

20. See Dennis, "To the Spectator, upon His Paper on the 16th of April," *Critical Works* 2:18–22.

21. See Elioseff, *Cultural Milieu*, pp. 75–76; Silas E. Summers, "Addison's Conception of Tragedy," *College English* 8 (1947):245–48; and Rothstein, *Restoration Tragedy*, p. 22, n. 29.

CHAPTER THREE: BURKE

1. *On the Sublime*, trans. William Smith (London, 1739), p. 140 (n. 3 on sec. 10). See also pp. 146–48 (n. 1 on sec. 15) for Smith's comment on *Macbeth* and the sublimity of horror; and Monk, *Sublime*, pp. 61–62, 68 (where Smith is quoted).

2. All references to the *Enquiry* will be to the edition ed. J. T. Boulton (London, 1958). The Editor's Introduction includes a helpful account of the sublime.

3. *The Works of the Right Honourable Edmund Burke*, 12 vols. (London, 1887), 3:333, 346–47, 352–53.

4. Richard Payne Knight, *An Analytical Inquiry into the Principles of Taste*, 2d ed. (London, 1805), pp. 59–60 (pt. 1, chap. 5, secs. 4–5). Cited in Hipple, *The Beautiful*, p. 92. See also *Enquiry*, Editor's Introduction, pp. lvi, lix.

5. B. Barrett, *Pretensions to a Final Analysis of the Nature and Origin of Sublimity, Style, Beauty, Genius, and Taste; with an Appendix Explaining the Causes of the Pleasure Which Is Derived from Tragedy* (London, 1812), Appendix, pp. 144–49. See also J. and A. L. Aikin, *Miscellaneous Pieces, in Prose* (London, 1773), pp. 123–25; James Beattie, *Dissertations Moral and Critical* (London, 1783), pp. 615–17; Knight, *Analytical Inquiry*, pp. 317–20 (3. 1. 4–7); Monk, *Sublime*, p. 130.

6. Anthony Ashley Cooper, 3d Earl of Shaftesbury, *Characteristicks of Men, Manners, Opinions, Times*, 4th ed., 3 vols. (London, 1727), 1:317–18; 2:106–107. See Wasserman, *ELH* 4:298.

7. In his "Introduction on Taste," Burke does allow the judgment a limited role in perceiving differences between an object and an imitation (*Enquiry*, pp. 17–18).

8. See my chap. 6, p. 85.

9. "A Short View of Tragedy," in *The Critical Works of Thomas Rymer*, ed. Curt A. Zimansky (New Haven, 1956), pp. xxix, 26, 27, 32, 201. Cited in Rothstein, *ELH* 29:307.

10. See my Introduction, p. 8.

11. *Lectures on Rhetoric and Belles Lettres* (New York, 1830), p. 516 (lect. 14).

12. Clifford Leech, *Shakespeare's Tragedies* (London, 1950), pp. 22–27.

13. *The Death of Tragedy* (New York, 1961), p. 4. See also Geoffrey Brereton, *Principles of Tragedy* (Coral Gables, Fla., 1968), pp. 109–10; T. R. Henn, *The Harvest of Tragedy* (New York, 1966), pp. 146–48.

14. Friedrich Nietzsche, *The Birth of Tragedy and The Genealogy of Morals*, trans. Francis Golffing (New York, 1956), pp. 19–20, 27, 62–63, 88–89, et passim.

15. *Shakespearean Tragedy* (London, 1960), p. 39. See also A. C. Bradley, "Hegel's Theory of Tragedy," *Oxford Lectures on Poetry*, 2d ed. (London, 1950), p. 85.

16. "Hegel's Theory of Tragedy," pp. 75, 90.

17. G. W. F. Hegel, *The Philosophy of Fine Art*, trans. F. P. B.

Osmaston, 4 vols. (London, 1920), 4:340–42. See Bradley's "Hegel's Theory of Tragedy," pp. 79–80.

18. "Hegel's Theory of Tragedy," p. 91.

19. See Brereton, *Principles,* pp. 117–18; and Henn, *Harvest,* pp. 26–27.

20. Philip Hobsbaum, " 'King Lear' in the Eighteenth Century," *Modern Language Review* 68 (1973):495.

21. George Campbell, *The Philosophy of Rhetoric* (New York, 1871), pp. 151–60; Henry Kirk White, *Remains,* 5th ed., 3 vols. (London, 1810), 2:2–5, 219; Blair, *Lectures,* p. 516; Wasserman, *ELH* 4:304–305. In *The Philosophy of Rhetoric* (1776) Campbell also summarizes and rejects four other explanations of the pleasure that arises from painful materials: distraction by strong excitement (Du Bos), moderation of pain by an awareness of fiction (Fontenelle), conversion of the painful through eloquence (Hume), and the vicarious enjoyment of suffering which we know we can end when we wish (Hobbes) (pp. 134–51 [bk. 1, chap. 9]).

22. Kames, *Elements of Criticism,* 2:372–78, esp. 377 (chap. 23). Cited by Wasserman, *ELH* 4:305. See also Blair, *Lectures,* pp. 515–16.

23. J. and A. L. Aikin, *Miscellaneous Pieces,* pp. 196–98.

24. [Arthur Murphy], *The Gray's-Inn Journal,* 2 vols. (London, 1756) 2:223. Cited by Hobsbaum, *MLR* 68:499.

25. See Carrol Fry, "The Concept of the Sublime in Eighteenth Century Gothic Fiction," *Mankato State College Studies* 1 (1966):31–44, esp. pp. 34–35; Malcolm Ware, *Sublimity in the Novels of Ann Radcliffe* (Upsala and Copenhagen, 1963). Cf. Knight, *Analytical Inquiry,* p. 393 (3. 1. 84).

26. "Johnson as Critic," *Scrutiny* 12 (1944):198. Cited by Hobsbaum, *MLR* 68:498.

27. See Hobsbaum, *MLR* 68:500–501.

CHAPTER FOUR: GERARD

1. See Wasserman, *ELH* 4:299–300: "The methods of refuting the earlier theories occasionally differed, Burke's explanation was occasionally modified, and sometimes it was blended with others; but it served Adam Smith, Hugh Blair, Lord Kames, George Walker, George Campbell, Lucy Aiken [*sic*],

Henry Kirke White, and many others," a number of whom are listed by Wasserman, pp. 300–301, n.

2. For both bibliographical and biographical details, see W. J. Hipple's Introduction to *An Essay on Taste . . . Facsimile Reproduction of the Third Edition (1780) . . .* (Gainesville, Florida, 1963), pp. v-xxviii. All references are to *An Essay on Taste,* 3d ed. (Edinburgh, 1780).

3. Hipple, *The Beautiful,* p. 82.

4. *An Essay on Taste,* pp. 1–2 (Introduction). Cf. Francis Hutcheson, *An Inquiry into the Original of Our Ideas of Beauty and Virtue,* 2d ed. (London, 1726), pp. 7–16 (bk. 1, chap. 1).

5. The imagination, for Gerard, does not include—as it does for Hobbes, Addison, and Hume—the recall of images "attended with remembrances" but only the amalgamation of ideas into new forms (pp. 151–53 [pt. 3, sec. 1]). Cf. *Leviathan,* pp. 8–10 (1. 2); *Spectator* 411; *A Treatise of Human Nature,* 1:9–10 (1. 3), 85–86 (3. 5).

6. See also Alexander Gerard, *An Essay on Genius 1774,* ed. Bernhard Fabian (München, 1966), pp. 39–41 (pt. 1, sec. 2); Hipple, *The Beautiful,* pp. 78–81; and Marjorie Grene, "Gerard's *Essay on Taste,*" *Modern Philology,* 40 (1943):45–60.

7. Baillie, *Essay on the Sublime,* pp. 10–11.

8. *Treatise,* 2:435–36 (3. 8). See my chap. 2, pp. 31–32.

9. In his section on "Grandeur and Sublimity" Gerard seems to exclude the linking of cause and effect from what he calls "association," but elsewhere in the *Essay on Taste* he uses the word "association" to include causal connections (pp. 153–54 [pt. 3, sec. 1]).

10. Cf. Monk, *Sublime,* p. 112.

11. Hartley, *Observations,* 2:244–45 (1. 2–3). See also 1:303ff.

12. In his *Essay on Genius* Gerard makes "judgment" the more general term, charging this faculty principally with comparison and discrimination. Reason, which is one kind of judgment, induces general principles and makes deductions therefrom (pp. 32–33 [1. 2]).

13. See also pp. 90–95 (2. 3); Grene, *MP* 40:56; and Hipple, *The Beautiful,* p. 80. According to Grene, Gerard establishes as the criterion for true taste "a more or less crystallized set of preferences serving as a standard for a limited

group of educated gentlemen" (p. 56). Hipple does not believe that Gerard erected "local and temporary prejudices into universal principles. The true principles are determined only by analyses of the mind. . . . Philosophical criticism, not universal consensus, is the only just test for new works or the work of obscure nations." "The real constitution of human nature" does not vary with time or place (pp. 80–81).

14. Once again Gerard draws on Hutcheson for his terms, designating the beauty peculiar to imitation as "relative" or "secondary," as distinguished from the "absolute" or "primary" beauty of actual objects (Hutcheson, *Inquiry*, pp. 16–29, 40–46 (1. 2).

15. David Hume, "Of Tragedy," *Essays, Moral, Political, and Literary,* ed. T. H. Green and T. H. Grose, 2 vols. (London, 1889), 2:261, 263–64.

16. See Ralph Cohen, "The Transformation of Passion: A Study of Hume's Theories of Tragedy," *Philological Quarterly* 41 (1962):450–64.

17. *Treatise,* 2:424 (1. 6). See also 2:373–74, 419–22, 439, 441 (2. 8; 3. 4, 6, 9).

18. See Hipple, *The Beautiful,* p. 70.

19. *Analytical Inquiry,* p. 328 (3. 1, 16).

20. F. L. Lucas, *Tragedy* (London, 1957), pp. 63–64.

21. Campbell, *Philosophy of Rhetoric,* pp. 144–45; White, *Remains,* 2:213–15. See Cohen, *PQ* 41:455; Wasserman, *ELH* 14:303, 303, n.

22. See chap. 3 on Burke.

23. J. and A. L. Aikin, *Miscellaneous Pieces,* pp. 196–201.

24. A. C. Bradley, "The Sublime," in *Oxford Lectures on Poetry,* 2d ed. (London, 1950), pp. 51–55. See Immanuel Kant, *Critique of Judgment,* trans. J. H. Bernard (New York, 1951), pp. 96–99 (pt. 1, div. 1, bk. 2, sec. 27); and my chap. 7, p. 101. See also Monk, *Sublime,* pp. 110–11.

CHAPTER FIVE: ALISON

1. Monk, *Sublime,* pp. 148–53, et passim. See also Hipple, *The Beautiful,* pp. 158–81.

2. See Martin Kallich, "The Meaning of Archibald Alison's *Essays on Taste,*" *Philological Quarterly* 27 (1948):314–24;

Francis Jeffrey, "Alison on Taste," *Contributions to the Edinburgh Review* (New York, 1969), pp. 13–39; Arthur Beatty, *William Wordsworth, His Doctrine and Art in Their Historical Relations*, 3d ed. (Madison, Wis., 1960), pp. 38, 45–51, 159.

3. All references will be to the edition of the *Essays* published in Boston in 1812, which is based on the Edinburgh edition of 1811.

4. *An Enquiry Concerning Human Understanding* (La Salle, Ill., 1938), pp. 21–22 (sec. 3). See Hipple, *The Beautiful*, pp. 168–69.

5. *Leviathan*, pp. 14–15 (1. 3); *Elements of Criticism*, 1:93 (chap. 2), 173 (chap. 2), 315 (chap. 9).

6. Kallich, *PQ* 27:315.

7. Sir Joshua Reynolds, *Discourses on Art*, ed. R. R. Wark (San Marino, Calif., 1959), pp. 230–34 (Discourse 13); Abraham Tucker, *The Light of Nature Pursued*, 2d ed., 7 vols. (London, 1805), 2:1–6.

8. *On the Sublime*, p. 75 (44). See Scott Elledge, "The Background and Development in English Criticism of the Theories of Generality and Particularity," *PMLA* 62 (1947): 147–82.

9. See my chap. 4, pp 56–57.

10. Samuel Johnson, *Works*, 11 vols. (Oxford, 1825), 7:16–17. See also *Rambler* 36, *Works*, 2:178; and Elledge, *PMLA* 62:160–68.

11. Kames, 2:397–98 (chap. 22), 407–409 (chap. 23); see also 1: 200–201 (chap. 3); and Ralph Cohen, "Association of Ideas and Poetic Unity," *Philological Quarterly* 36 (1957):465–74. Kames would also have the unities of time and place observed within each act (1:427–28 [chap. 23]).

12. See my chap. 4, pp. 64–65.

CHAPTER SIX: KNIGHT

1. Knight, *Analytical Inquiry*. Knight's organization, as Hipple has pointed out (*The Beautiful*, p. 270), recalls Hume's distinction between ideas and impressions and his division of impressions (which are livelier than ideas) into sensations and passions (*An Enquiry Concerning Human Understanding*, sec. 2, p. 15).

2. See my Introduction, p. 5.
3. See *Enquiry*, p. 47 (1. 15); and my chap. 3, p. 44.
4. Cf. *Enquiry*, pp. 39–40, 45–48, et passim (1.7, 14, 15); and my chap. 3, p. 44. For a fuller analysis, see Hipple, *The Beautiful*, pp. 272–74.
5. See my chap. 1, pp. 17–18.
6. See my chap. 1, p. 17.
7. See also p. 451 (3. 3. 25): "The end of morality is to restrain and subdue all the irregularities of passion and affection; and to subject the conduct of life to the dominion of abstract reason, and the uniformity of established rule: but the business of poetry, whether tragic or comic, whether epic or dramatic, is to display and even exaggerate those irregularities; and to exhibit the events of life diversified by all the wild varieties of ungoverned affections, or checquered by all the fantastic modes of anomalous and vitiated habits. It is, therefore, utterly impossible for the latter to afford models for the former; and, the instant that it attempts it, it necessarily becomes tame and vapid; and, in short, ceases to be poetry."
8. See also pp. 293, 402–405 (2. 3. 39–40; 3. 1. 92–94).

CHAPTER SEVEN: THE SUBLIME OF VISION

1. Blake, "Auguries of Innocence," *Complete Writings*, ed. Geoffrey Keynes (London, 1969), p. 431; "A Vision of the Last Judgment," Blake, p. 617. All references to Blake are to this edition.
2. *The Prelude* (1850 ed.), bk. 6, ll. 600–608, from the text in *The Prelude, or Growth of a Poet's Mind*, ed. E. de Selincourt and H. Darbishire, 2d ed. (Oxford, 1959), p. 209.
3. Coleridge, "Hymn before Sun-rise, in the Vale of Chamouni," ll. 13–16, in *Complete Poetical Works*, 2 vols., ed. E. H. Coleridge (Oxford, 1912), 1:377. Quoted in Morris, *Religious Sublime*, pp. 190–91.
4. Shelley, "Mont Blanc," ll. 37–40, 141–44, in *Complete Works* (Julian Edition), 10 vols., ed. R. Ingpen and W. E. Peck (London, 1927), 1:230, 233. All references to Shelley's *Complete Works* are to this edition.
5. Ll. 95–97, in *Poetical Works*, 2d ed., 5 vols., ed. E. de Selincourt and H. Darbishire (Oxford, 1952–1959), 2:262.

6. Letter to Thomas Butts, 6 July 1803, *Complete Writings,* p. 825.
7. Blake, *Complete Writings,* p. 457.
8. Ibid., p. 152.
9. *A Descriptive Catalog,* in Blake, *Complete Writings,* pp. 579–80. Cf. *The Four Zoas,* "Night the Second," ll. 33–34, Blake, p. 281.
10. Blake, *Complete Writings,* pp. 152, 305, 348, 377, 428, 484, 496, 500, 641, 715, 721, 731, 776, 795, et passim.
11. Annotations to Reynolds quoted in Blake, *Complete Writings,* pp. 457, 459, 464, 473, 476–77. See also "A Vision of the Last Judgment," Blake, p. 611, and Northrop Frye, *Fearful Symmetry* (Princeton, N.J., 1969), pp. 91–93. Cf. my chap. 3, p. 40. Blake uses the word "determinate," as Knight uses "distinct," for a quality that gives images a sharp outline but does not limit their power to excite the imagination.
12. Letter to Dr. Trusler, 23 Aug. 1799, Blake, *Complete Writings,* p. 393.
13. See Clarence DeWitt Thorpe, "Coleridge on the Sublime," in *Wordsworth and Coleridge: Studies in Honor of George McLean Harper,* ed. E. L. Griggs (Princeton, N.J., 1939), pp. 192–219.
14. From *Allsop's Letters, Conversations, and Recollections of S. T. Coleridge* (1836), in *Table Talk and Omniana* (London, 1917), pp. 442–43. Reprinted in *Biographia Literaria,* ed. J. Shawcross (Oxford, 1907), p. 309; and Thorpe, "Coleridge on the Sublime," pp. 195–96.
15. *Critique of Judgment,* pp. 96–99 (1. 1. 2. 27).
16. "Christmas Out of Doors," in *The Friend, The Collected Works of Samuel Taylor Coleridge,* ed. Barbara E. Rooke (London, 1969), vol. 4, pt. 1:367. See Thorpe, "Coleridge on the Sublime," pp. 196–99, 213–15.
17. J. Shawcross, "Coleridge's Marginalia," *Notes and Queries,* 10th Ser., 4 (1905):341–42. Quoted by Thorpe, "Coleridge on the Sublime," pp. 198–99.
18. "Christmas Out of Doors," p. 367. Cf. *Coleridge's Shakespearean Criticism,* ed. Thomas M. Raysor, 2d ed. (London, 1960), 2:103–104.
19. *Coleridge's Miscellaneous Criticism,* ed. T. M. Raysor (Cambridge, Mass., 1936), pp. 11–12. Quoted in Thorpe, "Coleridge on the Sublime," p. 207. Raysor notes Coleridge's

source in Schlegel's *Werke* (Böcking), 5:11–12. Cf. Hazlitt, "Schlegel on the Drama," *Complete Works* (16:60–62).

20. Letters to Josiah Wedgwood, 21 May(?) 1799, E. L. Griggs, ed., *Unpublished Letters of Samuel Taylor Coleridge* (New Haven, 1933), 1:117. Quoted in Thorpe, "Coleridge on the Sublime," p. 210.

21. Preface to the Edition of 1815, in *Poetical Works,* 2:439.

22. See Letter to John Thelwell, 17 Dec. 1796, *Letters of Samuel Taylor Coleridge,* ed. E. H. Coleridge (London, 1895), 2:197. Quoted in Thorpe, "Coleridge on the Sublime," p. 209.

23. Another tragedy, *The Fall of Robespierre,* was published under Coleridge's name in 1794. It represents the combined efforts of Coleridge, Southey, and Robert Lovell, with Southey probably doing most of it.

24. E.g., Osmond in M. G. Lewis, *The Castle Spectre* (London, 1798); and Adelmorn in M. G. Lewis, *Adelmorn, the Outlaw,* 2d ed. (London, 1801).

25. References to *The Borderers* are all to the text and notes in *The Poetical Works of William Wordsworth* (1:128–225; 341–49). The notes include Wordsworth's comments on the play and his prefatory essay to it.

26. For fuller accounts of *The Borderers,* and of *Osorio* and *Remorse* as well, see Bertrand Evans, *Gothic Drama from Walpole to Shelley* (Berkeley, 1947), pp. 216–24; and Richard M. Fletcher, *English Romantic Drama 1795–1843* (New York, 1966), pp. 34–69.

27. *The Dramas of Lord Byron* (New York, 1964), p. 28. Quoted in Fletcher, p. 54.

28. References to *Remorse* are to *The Complete Poetical Works of Samuel Taylor Coleridge,* 2:812–83.

29. See also 1. 2. 36–37; 3. 1. 21–30. Cf. *The Borderers,* act. 3, ll. 1440–47.

30. *Table Talk and Omniana,* 29 Dec. 1822, pp. 33–34. See also 16 Feb. 1833, p. 210. Quoted in Thorpe, "Coleridge on the Sublime," pp. 217–18. See also *Coleridge's Miscellaneous Criticism,* p. 263. "Othello's handkerchief," says Hazlitt (in 1816), "is not classical, . . . it is only a powerful instrument of passion and imagination (*Complete Works* 16:61).

31. *Table Talk and Omniana,* 3 May 1830, p. 91; 25 July 1832, p. 191 (quoted in Thorpe, "Coleridge on the Sublime," p.

208); *Coleridge's Miscellaneous Criticism,* p. 164 (quoted in Thorpe, p. 216).

32. See the 1815 Preface, *Poetical Works,* and the well-documented analysis in James Scoggins, *Imagination and Fancy, Complementary Modes in the Poetry of Wordsworth* (Lincoln, Neb., 1966), chap. 4, esp. pp. 149–59.
33. Preface to the Edition of 1815, *Poetical Works,* p. 439.
34. Scoggins, *Imagination,* pp. 139–71.
35. Dennis, *Critical Works,* 1:338–39.
36. Ibid., and J. A. W. Heffernan, *PMLA* 82 (1967):430–36. See also W. A. Madden, "The Victorian Sensibility," *Victorian Studies* 7 (1963):71–72; and my chap. 1, p. 19.
37. See also Scoggins, *Imagination,* pp. 168–90; Michael Irwin, "Wordsworth's 'Dependency Sublime,'" *Essays in Criticism* 14 (1964):352–62.
38. See Sigmund K. Proctor, *Thomas De Quincey's Theory of Literature* (Ann Arbor, Mich., 1943), pp. 81–86; and John E. Jordan, *Thomas De Quincey, Literary Critic* (Berkeley, Calif., 1952), pp. 55–68.
39. "On Milton," in *The Collected Writings of Thomas De Quincey,* 14 vols., ed. David Masson (Edinburgh, 1896–97), 5:401.
40. Ibid., pp. 400–402.
41. *Autobiography,* in *Collected Writings,* 2:72; "A Brief Appraisal of the Greek Literature," *Collected Writings,* 10:300. See also Proctor, *De Quincey's Theory,* pp. 84–86; Jordan, *Thomas De Quincey,* p. 58.
42. "Schlosser's Literary History," *Collected Writings,* 11:24. Quoted in Proctor, *De Quincey's Theory,* p. 87.
43. Preface to *Milton,* Blake, *Complete Writings,* p. 480.
44. Letter to Thomas Butts, 6 July 1803, Blake, *Complete Writings,* p. 825.
45. *A Descriptive Catalog,* Blake, *Complete Writings,* pp. 569–70, 572. See also Frye, *Fearful Symmetry,* p. 121.
46. *A Descriptive Catalog, Complete Writings,* p. 579.
47. Letter to John Flaxman, 12 Sept. 1800, Blake, *Complete Writings,* p. 799.
48. *A Descriptive Catalog, Complete Writings,* p. 569.
49. Blake, *Complete Writings,* p. 669 (plate 41, ll. 29–30).
50. *Fearful Symmetry,* p. 304.
51. *A Defence of Poetry, Complete Works,* 7:112.

52. Ibid.
53. See John Shawcross, Introduction to *Shelley's Literary and Philosophical Criticism* (London, 1909), p. xxvi.
54. Preface to *Prometheus Unbound, Complete Works,* 2:174–75. Quoted in Earl R. Wasserman, *Shelley: A Critical Reading* (Baltimore, Md., 1971) p. 101.
55. Dedication to *The Cenci, Complete Works,* 2:67.
56. Preface to *The Cenci, Complete Works,* 2:70.
57. To Charles Ollier, 6 Mar. 1820, *The Letters of Percy Bysshe Shelley,* 2 vols., ed. F. L. Jones (Oxford, 1964), 2:164. Quoted in Wasserman, *Shelley,* p. 102.
58. Preface to *The Cenci, Complete Works,* 2:70–73. See Wasserman, *Shelley,* p. 101.
59. See my chap. 3, p. 19.
60. *Defence of Poetry, Complete Works,* 7:122.
61. Ibid., pp. 119–20.
62. Preface to *The Cenci, Complete Works,* 2:70–71. Cf. Preface to *Prometheus Unbound, Complete Works,* 2:173.
63. Cf. Wasserman, *Shelley,* p. 94.
64. *Defence of Poetry, Complete Works,* 7:121.
65. For this analysis I am particularly indebted to Wasserman, *Shelley,* pp. 84–128 (chap. 3), and, for an evaluation of the imagery, to Stuart Curran, *Shelley's* Cenci (Princeton, N.J., 1970), pp. 97–128 (chap. 4).
66. "An Answer to the Question What Is Poetry?" prefatory essay to *Imagination or Fancy; or, Selections from the English Poets* (London, 1910), pp. 9, 26–28. The first two of Hunt's examples (*Antony and Cleopatra,* 4. 14. 3–14; and *King Lear,* 2. 4. 194) had both been cited by Hazlitt as showing the combining power of the imagination and its sublimity (1:25, n.; 16:63; 18:335). The third illustration (*Paradise Lost,* bk. 2, ll. 636–43) appears in Wordsworth's 1815 Preface as an example of imaginative power.
67. "An Answer to the Question What Is Poetry?," pp. 6, 27.

CHAPTER EIGHT: HAZLITT

1. All references to Hazlitt's writings will be to *The Complete Works of William Hazlitt,* ed. P. P. Howe, 21 vols. (London, 1830–34).
2. See J.-C. Sallé, "Hazlitt the Associationist," *Review of Eng-*

lish Studies, N.S. 15 (1964):38–51; Albrecht, *Creative Imagination,* pp. 12–14; 82–84.

3. *Discourses on Art,* pp. 230–34 (Discourse 13).

4. *The Light of Nature Pursued,* 2:1–6. See also [Hazlitt's] *An Abridgment of the Light of Nature Pursued* (London, 1807), pp. 81–84.

5. See also 1:21, 50–51; 4:260; 8:104; 12:46, 150–51; 20:72–73.

6. See also 5:47–48; 8:42–43; 20:369.

7. See Albrecht, *Creative Imagination,* pp. 68–69, 79–81. See also my Introduction, p. 10, and note 12 on Introduction.

8. *Enquiry,* pp. 40–42, 51, 113–17 (1. 8–10, 18; 3. 13–18).

9. Johnson, *Life of Cowley,* in *Works,* 7:16–17, 38. See also Hagstrum, *PMLA* 64:151; and Alex Page, "Faculty Psychology and Metaphor in Eighteenth-Century Criticism," *Modern Philology* 66 (1969):237–47, esp. 244.

10. See also 4:154; 5:6, 268–70.

11. Cf. Burke, *Enquiry,* pp. 45–46 (1. 14).

12. Cf. ibid., p. 47–48 (1. 15).

13. See 1:12, 251, 251, n., 305, 332–33; 7:102; 11:18–19; 12:46; 19:159–61, 305.

14. See Albrecht, *Creative Imagination,* esp. 26–28, 52–53, 59–62, 121–22; and Roy Park, *Hazlitt and the Spirit of the Age* (Oxford, 1971), esp. pp. 206–36.

15. And A. W. Schlegel. See my chap. 7, pp. 102–103.

16. See Herbert J. Muller, *The Spirit of Tragedy* (New York, 1956), pp. 182–84. According to George Steiner, "the fall of Troy is the first great metaphor of tragedy" (*Death of Tragedy,* p. 5).

17. See Brereton, pp. 92–94, 99; Hegel, 4:310, 331, 334–35, 337–38, 342; Robert M. Heilman, "To Know Himself: An Aspect of Tragic Structure," *Review of English Literature* 5 (1964): 36–56; William G. McCollum, *Tragedy* (New York, 1957), pp. 8–9, 23, 26, et passim; Muller, *Spirit of Tragedy,* pp. 191–92; Richard B. Sewall, *The Vision of Tragedy* (New Haven, Conn., 1959), pp. 74–79.

18. Nevertheless, Hazlitt's emphasis on the passionate moment tempted him to look at scenes rather than whole plays, even to forgive a poor play for a great scene. See Joseph W. Donohue, Jr., "Hazlitt's Sense of the Dramatic Actor as Tragic Character," *Studies in English Literature 1500–1900* 5 (1965):718–19.

19. See above, p. 101. No direct influence is likely. Hazlitt knew Kant only through commentators and had a poor opinion of him (1:128–29; 16:122–24). Bradley's paraphrase of Kant (see above pp. 67–68) is in terms that Hazlitt would have found more acceptable.

20. See "On the Tragedies of Shakespeare, Considered with Reference to Their Fitness for Stage Representation," in *The Works of Charles and Mary Lamb*, ed. E. V. Lucas (London, 1903), 1:107; and my chap. 9, p. 144.

21. Quoted by Donohue, *English Literature*, 5:718.

CHAPTER NINE: KEATS

1. Keats's debt to Hazlitt has been frequently explored. See W. J. Bate, *John Keats* (Cambridge, Mass., 1963), chap. 10, pp. 242–61; also R. T. Davies, "Keats and Hazlitt," *Keats-Shelley Memorial Bulletin* 13 (1957):1–8; Kenneth Muir, "Keats and Hazlitt," *Proceedings of the Leeds Philosophical and Literary Society, Literary and Historical Sections* 6 (1951):534–50; Herschel M. Sikes, "The Poetic Theory and Practice of Keats: The Record of a Debt to Hazlitt," *Philological Quarterly* 38 (1959):401–12.

2. This and references not otherwise designated in the text are to *The Letters of John Keats 1814–1821*, ed. H. E. Rollins (Cambridge, Mass., 1958), 2 vols.

3. *Leviathan*, pp. 14–15 (1. 4).

4. For occurrences of the word *truth* in Keats's prose writings, see Newell J. Ford, *The Prefigurative Imagination of John Keats* (Hamden, Conn., 1966), p. 161.

5. Ibid., p. 149.

6. *The Concordance to the Poetry of John Keats*, ed. D. L. Baldwin, J. W. Hebel, et al. (Washington, D.C., 1917), lists eight appearances: three in *Endymion* (bk. 3, ll. 329, 965; bk. 4, l. 331), one in "To J. H. Reynolds," (l. 69; also in *Letters*, 1:261), one in *The Fall of Hyperion* (canto 1, l. 173), two in *The Cap and Bells* (st. 11, l. 8; st. 71, l. 9), and one in "Ode to Apollo" (l. 3). I have counted thirteen more occurrences in the letters: 1:*173*, *184*, 200, *261*, 304, 322, *325*, 387, *398* (2), *403* (2); 2:*94*. The italicized page numbers indicate what seem to be the more specific uses of the word.

For the texts of Keats's poems I have used *The Poetical Works of John Keats,* ed. H. W. Garrod (London, 1956).

7. *Keats the Poet* (Princeton, N.J., 1973), p. 126.
8. Cf. my chap. 2, pp. 31–32.
9. Sperry, *Keats the Poet,* cites among others the following: Sir Humphry Davy, *Elements of Chemical Philosophy,* in *The Collected Works of Sir Humphry Davy,* ed. John Davy (London, 1839–1840), 4:45–46, 140; William Nicholson, *First Principles of Chemistry,* 2d ed. (London 1792), pp. 34–35, 466; Andrew Ure, *A Dictionary of Chemistry* (1st American ed.; Philadelphia, 1821), "Abstraction," "Distillation," "Essences," "Evaporation," "Sublimation." See also *OED* for each of the terms defined above; and, for "ethereal," see Ford, *Prefigurative Imagination,* pp. 35, 53, 55, 161–62.
10. My italics.
11. See also 1:184.
12. The closing words are quoted inaccurately from Shelley's "Hymn to Intellectual Beauty," ll. 13–14.
13. See Ford, *Prefigurative Imagination,* p. 155 and 155, n.; also, for a list of occurrences of *speculation* in Keats's prose writings, pp. 161–62.
14. As Bate, *John Keats,* points out (p. 262), all of Keats's underscorings and annotations, with the exception of a note on *The Tempest,* appear in the essay on *Lear.* Keats's markings are printed in Amy Lowell, *John Keats,* 2 vols. (Boston, 1925), 2:587–90, and in the Hampstead Keats, 5:280–86.
15. See my chap. 8, p. 122.
16. "By 'philosophy' [Keats] does not mean metaphysics but knowledge and the fruits of reading generally" (see Sir Sidney Colvin, *John Keats, His Life and Poetry* [London, 1968], pp. 161–62).
17. See Earl R. Wasserman, *The Finer Tone* (Baltimore, 1953), pp. 16ff.
18. For a full account of *Otho the Great* and *King Stephen* see Bernice Slote, *Keats and the Dramatic Principle* (Lincoln, Neb., 1958), pp. 104–20. See also Bate, *John Keats,* pp. 562–68.
19. See esp. Bate, *John Keats,* pp. 585–605.
20. For the ambiguity of "dreamer," see J. M. Murry, *Keats,* 4th ed. (New York, 1955), pp. 242–43; and Sperry, *Keats the Poet,* p. 328.

21. It is in this sense that the unselfing in Keats's "Pleasure Thermometer" appears to be his "first Step towards the chief Attempt in the Drama" (1:218–19). Cf. Bate, *John Keats,* pp. 183–84.
22. See Sperry, *Keats the Poet,* pp. 314–16.

CHAPTER TEN: "THE FIERCE DISPUTE"

1. *The Visionary Company* (Ithaca, N.Y., 1971), p. xvii.
2. *Principles of Tragedy* (Coral Gables, Fla., 1968), p. 74.
3. *The Function of Criticism at the Present Time,* in *Lectures and Essays in Criticism,* in *Complete Prose Works,* ed. R. H. Super, 9 vols. (Ann Arbor, Mich., 1960–73), 3:265–66.
4. See especially *The Spirit of the Age* and "What Is the People?" in *Political Essays* (7:259–81).
5. *Tragedy: Serious Drama in Relation to Aristotle's Poetics* (London, 1957), p. 78.

BIBLIOGRAPHY

PRIMARY SOURCES

Addison, Joseph. *The Spectator*. Ed. Donald F. Bond. 5 vols. Oxford, 1965.

——. *Works*. Ed. George Washington Greene. 6 vols. Philadelphia, 1876–80.

Akenside, Mark. *Poetical Works*. Ed. Alexander Dyce. London, 1894.

Aikin, J. and A. L. *Miscellaneous Pieces, in Prose*. London, 1773.

Alison, Archibald. *Essays on the Nature and Principles of Taste*. Boston, 1812.

Arnold, Matthew. *The Function of Criticism at the Present Time*. In *Lectures and Essays in Criticism, Complete Prose Works*, ed. R. H. Super. 9 vols. Ann Arbor, Mich., 1960–73.

Baillie, [John]. *An Essay on the Sublime* (1747). Augustan Reprint Society. Los Angeles, 1953.

Barrett, B[asil R.]. *Pretensions to a Final Analysis of the Nature and Origin of Sublimity, Style, Beauty, Genius and Taste; with an Appendix Explaining the Causes of the Pleasure Which is Derived from Tragedy*. London, 1812.

Beattie, James. *Dissertations Moral and Critical*. London, 1783.

Bibliography

Blair, Hugh. *Lectures on Rhetoric and Belles Lettres.* New York, 1830.

Blake, William. *Complete Writings.* Ed. Geoffrey Keynes. London, 1969.

Boileau[-Despréaux, Nicolas]. *Traité du sublime, ou du Merveilleux dans le discours,* in *Oeuvres complètes.* Ed. Françoise Escal. Bruges, 1966. Pp. 331–440.

Burke, Edmund. *A Philosophical Enquiry into the Origin of Our Ideas of the Sublime and Beautiful.* Ed. J. T. Boulton, London, 1958.

———. *The Works of the Right Honourable Edmund Burke.* 12 vols. London, 1887.

[Burnet, Thomas]. *An Answer to the Exceptions Made by Mr. Erasmus Warren against the Sacred Theory of the Earth.* 3d ed. London, 1722.

[———]. *The Sacred Theory of the Earth.* 5th ed. 2 vols. London, 1722.

Campbell, George. *The Philosophy of Rhetoric.* New York, 1871.

Coleridge, Samuel Taylor. *Biographia Literaria.* Ed. J. Shawcross. Oxford, 1907.

———. *Coleridge's Miscellaneous Criticism.* Ed. Thomas M. Raysor. Cambridge, Mass., 1936.

———. *Complete Poetical Works.* Ed. Ernest Hartley Coleridge. 2 vols. Oxford, 1912.

———. *Letters.* Ed. Ernest Hartley Coleridge. 2 vols. Boston, 1895.

———. *Coleridge's Shakespearean Criticism.* Ed. Thomas M. Raysor. 2d ed. 2 vols. London, 1960.

———. *The Friend.* In *The Collected Works of Samuel Taylor Coleridge,* ed. Barbara E. Rooke. Vol. 4, part 1. London, 1969.

———. *Table Talk and Omniana.* London, 1917.

———. *Unpublished Letters of Samuel Taylor Coleridge.* Ed. Earl Leslie Griggs. 2 vols. New Haven, Conn., 1933.

Davy, Sir Humphry. *Elements of Chemical Philosophy.* In *The Collected Works of Sir Humphry Davy,* ed. John Davy. Vol. 4. London, 1839–40.

Dennis, John. *Critical Works.* Ed. Edward Hooker. 2 vols. Baltimore, 1939–43.

De Quincey, Thomas. *Collected Writings*. Ed. David Masson. 14 vols. Edinburgh, 1896–97.

Descartes, [René]. *Oeuvres*. Ed. Victor Cousin. 11 vols. Paris, 1824.

Dryden, John. *Essays*. Ed. W. P. Ker. 2 vols. New York, 1961.

Du Bos, [Jean-Baptiste]. *Refléxions critique sur la poésie et sur la peinture*. 5th ed. 3 vols. Paris, 1746.

Fontenelle, [Bernard Le Bovier de]. *Oeuvres*. 10 vols. Paris, 1758.

Gerard, Alexander. *An Essay on Genius 1774*. Ed. Bernhard Fabian. München, 1966.

———. *An Essay on Taste*. 3d ed. Edinburgh, 1780.

Hartley, David. *Observations on Man, His Frame, His Duty, and His Expectations*. 4th ed. 3 vols. London, 1801.

Hazlitt, William. *Complete Works*. Ed. P. P. Howe. 21 vols. London, 1930–34.

Hegel, G. W. F. *The Philosophy of Fine Art*. Trans. F. P. B. Osmaston. 4 vols. London, 1920.

Hobbes, Thomas. *Leviathan*. Ed. Michael Oakeshott. Oxford, 1957.

Hume, David. *An Enquiry Concerning Human Understanding*. La Salle, Ill., 1938.

———. *Essays, Morals, Political, and Literary*. Ed. T. H. Green and T. H. Grose. 2 vols. London, 1889.

———. *A Treatise of Human Nature*. Ed. L. A. Selby-Bigge. 2 vols. London, 1896.

Hunt, Leigh. *Imagination and Fancy; or, Selections from the English Poets*. 2 vols. London, 1910.

Hutcheson, Francis. *An Inquiry into the Original of Our Ideas of Beauty and Virtue*. 2d ed. London, 1726.

Jeffrey, Francis. *Contributions to the Edinburgh Review*. New York, 1869.

Johnson, Samuel. *Johnson on Shakespeare*. Ed. Arthur Sherbo. The Yale Edition of the *Works of Samuel Johnson*, vols. 7 and 8. New Haven, Conn., 1968.

———. *Works*. 11 vols. Oxford, 1825.

Kames, Henry Home, Lord. *Elements of Criticism*. 6th ed. 2 vols. Edinburgh, 1785.

Kant, Immanuel. *Critique of Judgment*. Trans. J. H. Bernard. New York, 1951.

Keats, John. *Letters 1814–1821.* Ed. Hyder E. Rollins. 2 vols. Cambridge, Mass., 1958.

———. *Poetical Works and Other Writings.* Ed. H. Buxton Forman and Maurice Buxton Forman. Hampstead Edition. 8 vols. New York, 1938–39.

———. *The Poetical Works.* Ed. H. W. Garrod. London, 1956.

Knight, Richard Payne. *An Analytical Inquiry into the Principles of Taste.* 2d ed. London, 1805.

Lamb, Charles and Mary. *Works.* Ed. E. V. Lucas. 7 vols. London, 1903.

Lewis, M[atthew] G[regory]. *The Castle Spectre: A Drama In Five Acts.* London, 1798.

———. *Adelmorn, the Outlaw; a Romantic Drama in Three Acts.* 2d ed. London, 1801.

Locke, John. *An Essay Concerning Human Understanding.* Ed. Alexander Campbell Fraser. 2 vols. Oxford, 1894.

Longinus, [Cassius]. *On the Sublime.* Trans. William Smith. London, 1739.

———. *On the Sublime: An English Translation by Benedict Einarson . . . and Sir Joshua Reynolds, Discourses on Art.* Introduction by Elder Olson. Chicago, 1945.

[Murphy, Arthur.] *The Gray's-Inn Journal.* 2 vols. London, 1756.

Nicholson, William. *The First Principles of Chemistry.* 3d ed. London, 1796.

Rapin, R[ené]. *Reflections on Aristotle's Treatise of Poesie.* London, 1674.

Reynolds, Sir Joshua. *Discourses on Art.* Ed. R. R. Wark. San Marino, Calif. 1959.

Rymer, Thomas. *Critical Works.* Ed. Curt A. Zimansky. New Haven, Conn., 1956.

Shaftesbury, Anthony Ashley Cooper, 3d Earl of. *Characteristicks of Men, Manners, Opinions, Times.* 4th ed. 3 vols. [London], 1727.

Shelley, Percy Bysshe. *Complete Works.* Ed. Roger Ingpen and Walter E. Peck. Julian Edition. 10 vols. London, 1927–30.

———. *Letters.* Ed. Frederick L. Jones. 2 vols. Oxford, 1964.

———. *Shelley's Literary and Philosophical Criticism.* Ed. John Shawcross. London, 1909.

Tucker, Abraham. *An Abridgment of the Light of Nature Pursued.* [Abridged by William Hazlitt]. London, 1807.

————. *The Light of Nature Pursued.* 2d ed. 7 vols. London, 1805.

Ure, Andrew. *A Dictionary of Chemistry.* 1st American ed. Philadelphia, 1821.

White, Henry Kirke. *Remains . . . with an Account of His Life by Robert Southey.* 5th ed. 3 vols. London, 1811.

Wordsworth, William. *Poetical Works.* Ed. Ernest de Selincourt and Helen Darbishire. 2d ed. 5 vols. Oxford, 1952–59.

————. *The Prelude, or Growth of a Poet's Mind.* Ed. Ernest de Selincourt and Helen Darbishire. 2d ed. Oxford, 1959.

Wordsworth, William and Dorothy. *Letters: The Middle Years.* Ed. Ernest de Selincourt. 2 vols. Oxford, 1937.

SECONDARY SOURCES

Albrecht, W. P. *Hazlitt and the Creative Imagination.* Lawrence, Kans., 1965.

Baldwin, D. L., J. W. Hebel, et al., eds. *The Concordance to the Poetry of John Keats.* Washington, D.C., 1917.

Bate, Walter Jackson. *John Keats.* Cambridge, Mass., 1963.

Beatty, Arthur. *William Wordsworth, His Doctrine and Art in Their Historical Relations.* 3d ed. Madison, Wis., 1960.

Bloom, Edward A. and Lillian D. "Addison on 'Moral Habits of the Mind.'" *Journal of the History of Ideas* 21 (1960):409–27.

Bloom, Harold. *The Visionary Company.* Ithaca, N.Y., 1971.

Bradley, A. C. *Oxford Lectures on Poetry.* 2d ed. London, 1950.

————. *Shakespearean Tragedy.* London, 1960.

Brereton, Geoffrey. *Principles of Tragedy, A Rational Examination of the Tragic Concept in Life and Literature.* Coral Gables, Fla., 1968.

Chew, Samuel C. *The Dramas of Lord Byron: A Critical Study.* New York, 1964. [First published 1915.]

Cohen, Ralph. "Association of Ideas and Poetic Unity." *Philological Quarterly* 36 (1957):465–75.

————. "The Transformation of Passion: A Study of Hume's Theories of Tragedy." *Philological Quaterly* 41 (1962):450–64.

Colvin, Sir Sidney. *John Keats, His Life and Poetry, His Friends, Critics, and After-Fame.* New York, 1917.

Bibliography

C[rane], R. S. Review of Monk, *The Sublime. Philological Quarterly* 15 (1936):165–67.

Curran, Stuart. *Shelley's Cenci: Scorpions Ringed with Fire.* Princeton, N.J., 1970.

Davies, R. T. "Keats and Hazlitt." *Keats-Shelley Memorial Bulletin* 13 (1957):1–8.

Donohue, Joseph W., Jr. "Hazlitt's Sense of the Dramatic Actor as Tragic Character." *Studies in English Literature 1500–1900* 5 (1965):701–21.

Elioseff, Lee Andrew. *The Critical Milieu of Addison's Literary Criticism.* Austin, Tex., 1963.

Elledge, Scott. "The Background and Development in English Criticism of the Theories of Generality and Particularity." *PMLA* 62 (1947):147–82.

Evans, Bertrand. *Gothic Drama from Walpole to Shelley.* Berkeley, Calif., 1947.

Fletcher, Richard M. *English Romantic Drama 1795–1843: A Critical History.* New York, 1966.

Ford, Newell F. *The Prefigurative Imagination of John Keats.* Hamden, Conn., 1966.

Fry, Carrol. "The Concept of the Sublime in Eighteenth Century Gothic Fiction." *Mankato State College Studies* 1 (1966): 31–34.

Frye, Northrop. *Fearful Symmetry, A Study of William Blake.* Princeton, N.J., 1969.

Grene, Marjorie. "Gerard's *Essay on Taste.*" *Modern Philology* 40 (1943):45–50.

Hagstrum, J. H. "Johnson's Conception of the Beautiful, the Pathetic, and the Sublime." *PMLA* 64 (1949):134–57.

Hathaway, Baxter. "The Lucretion 'Return upon Ourselves' in Eighteenth Century Theories of Tragedy." *PMLA* 62 (1947): 672–89.

Heffernan, James A. W. "Wordsworth and Dennis: The Discrimination of Feelings." *PMLA* 82 (1967):430–36.

Heilman, Robert B. "To Know Himself: An Aspect of Tragic Structure." *Review of English Literature* 5 (1964):36–56.

Henn, T. R. *The Harvest of Tragedy.* New York, 1966.

Hipple, Walter J., Jr. *The Beautiful, the Sublime, and the Picturesque in Eighteenth-Century British Aesthetic Theory.* Carbondale, Ill., 1957.

———. Introduction to Alexander Gerard, *An Essay on Taste*

. . . *Facsimile Reproduction of the Third Edition* (1780). Gainesville, Fla., 1963.

Hobsbaum, Philip. " 'King Lear' in the Eighteenth Century." *Modern Language Review* 68 (1973):494–506.

Irwin, Michael. "Wordsworth's 'Dependency Sublime.' " *Essays in Criticism* 14 (1964):352–62.

Jordan, John. *Thomas De Quincey, Literary Critic.* Berkeley, Calif., 1952.

Kallich, Martin. "The Meaning of Archibald Alison's *Essays on Taste.*" *Philological Quarterly* 27 (1948):314–24.

Krook, Dorothea. *Elements of Tragedy.* New Haven, Conn., 1969.

Leavis, F. R. "Johnson as Critic." *Scrutiny* 12 (1944):187–204.

Leech, Clifford. *Shakespeare's Tragedies.* London, 1950.

Lowell, Amy. *John Keats.* 2 vols. Boston, 1925.

Lucas, F. L. *Tragedy: Serious Drama in Relation to Aristotle's Poetics.* London, 1957.

Madden, William A. "The Victorian Sensibility." *Victorian Studies* 7 (1963):71–72.

Marsh, Robert. "Akenside and Addison: The Problem of Ideational Debt." *Modern Philology* 59 (1961):36–48.

McCollum, William G. *Tragedy.* New York, 1957.

Monk, Samuel. *The Sublime: A Study of Critical Theories in XVIII-Century England.* Ann Arbor, Mich., 1960.

Morris, David B. *The Religious Sublime: Christian Poetry and the Critical Tradition in 18th-Century England.* Lexington, Ky., 1972.

Muir, Kenneth. "Keats and Hazlitt." *Proceedings of the Leeds Philosophical and Literary Society, Literary and Historical Sections* 6 (1951):534–50.

Muller, Herbert J. *The Spirit of Tragedy.* New York, 1956.

Murry, John Middleton. *Keats.* 4th ed. New York, 1955.

Nicolson, Marjorie. *Mountain Gloom and Mountain Glory.* Ithaca, N.Y., 1959.

Nietzsche, Friedrich. *The Birth of Tragedy and the Genealogy of Morals.* Trans. Francis Golffing. New York, 1956.

Page, Alex. "Faculty Psychology and Metaphor in Eighteenth-Century Criticism." *Modern Philology* 66 (1969):237–47.

Park, Roy. *Hazlitt and the Spirit of the Age.* Oxford, 1971.

Proctor, Sigmund K. *Thomas De Quincey's Theory of Literature.* Ann Arbor, Mich., 1943.

197

Rothstein, Eric. "English Tragic Theory in the Late Seventeenth Century." *ELH* 29 (1962):306–23.

———. *Restoration Tragedy, Form and the Process of Change.* Madison, Wis., 1967.

Sallé, J.-C. "Hazlitt the Associationist." *Review of English Studies.* New Series, 15 (1964):38–51.

Scoggins, James. *Imagination and Fancy, Complementary Modes in the Poetry of Wordsworth.* Lincoln, Neb., 1966.

Sewall, Richard B. *The Vision of Tragedy.* New Haven, Conn., 1959.

Shawcross, J. "Coleridge's Marginalia." *Notes and Queries.* 10th series, 4 (1905):341–42.

Sikes, Herschel M. "The Poetic Theory and Practice of Keats: The Record of a Debt to Hazlitt." *Philological Quarterly* 38 (1958):401–402.

Slote, Bernice. *Keats and the Dramatic Principle.* Lincoln, Neb., 1958.

Spencer, Jeffrey B. *Heroic Nature: Ideal Landscape in English Poetry from Marvell to Thomson.* Evanston, Ill., 1973.

Sperry, Stuart M. *Keats the Poet.* Princeton, N.J., 1973.

Steiner, George. *The Death of Tragedy.* New York, 1961.

Summers, Silas E. "Addison's Conception of Tragedy." *College English* 8 (1947):245–48.

Thorpe, Clarence De Witt. "Addison's Contribution to Criticism." In Richard Foster Jones, et al., *The Seventeenth Century: Studies in the History of English Thought and Literature from Bacon to Pope,* pp. 316–29. Stanford, Calif., 1951.

———. "Addison's Theory of the Imagination as 'Perceptive Response.'" *Papers of the Michigan Academy of Science, Arts, and Letters* 21 (1935):509–30.

———. *The Aesthetic Theory of Thomas Hobbes.* Ann Arbor, Mich., 1940.

———. "Coleridge on the Sublime." In *Wordsworth and Coleridge: Studies in Honor of George McLean Harper,* ed. Earl Leslie Griggs, pp. 192–219. Princeton, N.J., 1939.

Trawick, Leonard M., III. "Hazlitt, Reynolds, and the Ideal." *Studies in Romanticism* 4 (1965):240–47.

Tuveson, Ernest. *Imagination as a Means of Grace.* Berkeley, Calif., 1960.

———. "Space, Deity, and the 'Natural Sublime.'" *Modern Language Quarterly* 12 (1951):20–38.

Ware, Malcolm. *Sublimity in the Novels of Ann Radcliffe.* Essays and Studies on English Language and Literature, No. 25. Upsala and Copenhagen, 1963.

Wasserman, Earl R. *The Finer Tone.* Baltimore, 1953.

———. "The Pleasures of Tragedy." *ELH* 14 (1947):283–307.

———. *Shelley: A Critical Reading.* Baltimore, 1971.

INDEX